COOKING

FAST

AND

SLOW

COOKING

FAST

AND

SLOW

NATALIA

RUDIN

Easy, comforting, (mostly) plant-based recipes for busy people

TEN SPEED PRESS
California | New York

For my amazing Mumma,
I would be nowhere without you.
Thank you for everything.

INTRODUCTION

I grew up in a foodie family. Most of my childhood was spent in London and almost all our meals were homemade from scratch, each lovingly cooked by my mother. Her food was strongly influenced by Austrian and Italian cuisine, both places where she spent her younger years traveling. Some of my favorite things to eat as a child were bolognese and a good Wiener schnitzel, and my mum's were always the best. My father was a huge advocate for trying new things and not being afraid of the unknown. He would always be ordering the wildest items on the menu, like snails, frog legs, or ox tongue, things I was totally terrified of trying as a child! I am half Russian on my father's side and my babushka perfectly fit the stereotype of being a feeder and showing her love through food. On our visits to Russia, she would ply me with blinis and homemade raspberry compote to my heart's content (the recipe for which is on page 186). This was all the perfect concoction to spark my interest in the culinary world. At age seven, I made what my oldest brother, Tom, called "the best omelet he had ever tasted." It was simple: eggs and a sprinkling of whatever cheese we had lurking in the fridge, but it came out perfectly. The kitchen was a mess, but I stood proudly among it, and there my love for cooking was born.

While I was young and still in school, I eased myself into cooking with simple savory recipes, which I often revert to now—things like bolognese sauce, penne pomodoro made from scratch, and tricolor salads. I'll never forget when I discovered balsamic glaze; it made me feel like a Michelin-starred chef, making abstract drizzles across plates of Parma ham, tomatoes, mozzarella, and figs. I quickly became obsessed with baking and would often be found with greasy butterfingers and covered in flour on weekends. Admittedly, for a long time it was a lot of Betty Crocker cake mix and store-bought frosting, but eventually I took the plunge and started making things from scratch. Very brown bananas were always a prompt and banana muffins were quite often piled up on a plate, displayed in our kitchen, and offered to any soul who passed through the front door. It wasn't until later, when I traveled around Southeast Asia, South and Central America, and India, that my horizons broadened in terms of cooking. I was introduced to herbs and spices I had never heard of and cooking methods that were completely foreign to me. I was in awe.

My childhood, although rich with travel and culture, was a little bit capricious. When I was seventeen, my parents divorced and things got a lot messier, including my state of mind. After a few years of binge-drinking, partying, and just general rebelling, I decided to travel solo around East Asia. I learned the value in nourishing my body, which in turn nourished my mind. Ingredients like lentils, beans, and chickpeas paired with a variety of colorful vegetables and spices became my new diet. (Not to say that my diet prior to that was terrible, just limited.) Indian cuisine had never really been a part of my life until I went there myself, and I quickly fell in love with the flavors of turmeric, cumin, and coriander. Learning about those ingredients inspired me to explore more of the culinary delights of places outside of Europe, such as the Middle East and Asia, using ingredients like gochujang, sumac, za'atar, and harissa, to name a few. The clear correlation between eating well and feeling well led me to realize what I wanted to do with my future. Cook. But not just for myself; I wanted to show people the importance of unprocessed foods and colorful ingredients, and the benefit they could have on your well-being. And so began my career as a personal chef.

With no professional training and very little experience, I knew finding my first client would be a challenge. Having practiced yoga and exercised almost every day, it became clear that these two aspects needed to be involved in my work. My unique selling point became that I could offer you a "retreat experience" at home. I found that people would often go on week-long retreats, leaving their kids, dogs, partners, and jobs at home, to eat well, sleep well, and exercise. Although these retreats were wonderful and would definitely have some sort of impact on their clients' daily habits, people would always fall off the wagon eventually—because life just does get in the way. Whether it's driving the kids to school, going to meetings, or walking the dog, our busy lives mean that healthy habits are often hard to keep up when you haven't been able to ingrain them into your normal life. My approach was to work around your normal day and fit everything in with ease, showing you how you can organize your new schedule so it merges seamlessly with your old one.

In 2018, I pretty much pestered my first client over email into giving me a job. We worked together for five weeks, set some goals on day one, and every single target was hit. I felt so fulfilled and relieved; starting this had been a big leap of faith. It could have easily gone horribly wrong, but seeing the joy and contentment it brought my client cemented the notion that this was what I needed to be doing. From there things snowballed—word of mouth was an amazing thing for me— and alongside work I studied to obtain a diploma as a health and nutrition coach and completed a 200-hour yoga teacher training. In February 2019, I set up my Instagram account, @natsnourishments, figuring that as I was making all this delicious healthy food, I may as well document it. This was absolutely terrifying at the time but totally worth it in the end.

For the last five years, I have worked with many different clients and been lucky enough to travel all over the world with them, getting to experience cuisines and ingredients intimately. The highs and lows were extraordinary. I remember the first time I secured a job in the Bahamas; I couldn't believe my luck. The clients were a lovely couple who lived in the most gorgeous house, and I had my own little apartment (it was actually very big, but little compared to the main house). The first time I was alone in my room I squealed with joy and jumped on the bed like a child, taking it all in. On my days off I would casually wander on the beach, and during working hours I had access to the best of the best kitchenware and tropical ingredients—all while getting paid to be there! The area where I was working was very much a community and my name spread like wildfire. Over the course of my career, I worked with several different clients in the Bahamas, some of them becoming repeat clients I would go back to every year. I would go from cooking dinner parties for up to twenty people to an intimate dinner for one or two. I made some really, really good friends, got invited to the most incredible parties and luxurious boat days, and even got to tag along to a private island in the Exumas for a week. I was also lucky enough to work with an incredible woman in Toronto. I was immediately welcomed into the family, invited to a countryside cottage, which was in fact much more akin to a manor house, and shown all the nicest parts of town.

The highs were very high, but the lows were also extremely low. As 2020 arrived, bringing Covid along with it, my business came to a crushing halt. I lost all my jobs and income overnight and became a sitting duck in London. I tried and failed to book flights, trains, anything that would take me back to work. Each attempt was unsuccessful and resulted in me losing more money and gaining more anxiety. My friends were able to either work from home or spend time frolicking in their gardens or parks while still being paid by their employer, yet there I was panicking that I would never work again. I remember reading an article in *Forbes* magazine, claiming that as an entrepreneur, the first two years of business were the hardest and if you didn't make it through, you were likely to never make it. This sent me into a spiral; I was sure this was it for me. I lost all my clients and my momentum was gone. Eventually, however, the negativity began to spur me on; after a few weeks of sulking and wishfully thinking that Covid would blow over and I would be back to work in no time, reality set in. Borders were closed and no one wanted me in their house. I needed to dig deep and be resourceful to try and support myself.

I had roughly 3,000 followers on Instagram at the time, so I put word out that I was providing a "meals on wheels" kind of service and—thankfully—a few people decided to take me on. I was preparing breakfasts, lunches, dinners, and snacks for up to ten people a week, as well as delivering most of them myself, in gloves and a mask, of course. It ended up being the busiest, most intense time of my career. I was run ragged but I loved it. My partner (now fiancé), Cameron, was my saving grace. He made sure I was eating properly and would pick up the housework I just didn't have the time or energy to do. Each night I would hit the pillow and be asleep within minutes. I set up a website and began selling granola, cookies, and other baked goods, which kept me incredibly busy. As Covid prolonged but rules loosened (slightly), I was hired to cater for six-person dinner parties. Restaurants were closed and takeout wasn't quite as glamorous as what some people wanted. I would precook all the food at home, drive to people's houses, set it all up nicely, and then leave. When the world opened back up again, I went back to private cheffing and only did dinner parties in between jobs, to keep things running slowly but steadily.

My job has thrown me into all sorts of situations, from thinking on my feet to prepare a delicious meal on extremely short notice, to feeding fussy children, entertaining twenty-plus guests, and accommodating the most restrictive dietary requirements. All these experiences have allowed me to accumulate a sort of mental recipe bank for each occasion, which I wish to share with you.

As a personal chef, the requirement was not always to create high-end dishes that look like they've come from a Michelin-starred restaurant, but more to provide home-cooked meals for those who couldn't (or didn't want to) do it themselves. Obviously, for dinner parties and big occasions, things would be quite special, but for everyday meals my clients just wanted hearty, wholesome, healthy food that they could enjoy with the family or curl up on the sofa with—simple dishes with a few elevations one might not think of. Before starting a new job with a client, I would send a questionnaire that would give me insight to their allergies, intolerances, likes, and dislikes. This made it easy to proceed with menus, as most of the time it was up to me what was going to be eaten. The first week would always be quite nerve-racking as you were sussing out someone's palate, but after a few meals you get to know their preferences and adjust your style of cooking to them. It then just becomes second nature.

It was such an all-consuming and tiring job that when it came to feeding myself, I often risked falling into bad habits. Usually, while at work, I would have little tasters of a lot of food throughout the day, and by the time I got home, I wasn't motivated to cook for myself. It was rare that I would eat three proper meals a day. But after a while, I realized I needed meals that would fill me up and keep me energized and nourished. I started to create a roster of quick, simple, and nourishing recipes that ensured I was eating well at the end of each day, which is what we all need, right?

My Nat's Nourishments Instagram account was a quiet little machine running in the background, so on weekends I would often spend most of my time cooking, filming, and shooting three or four recipes so that during the week I had enough content to post to try and keep up with the algorithms. I was fairly inconsistent with this. It was hard to maintain as I was spending a lot of time away from home and in clients' houses, where I couldn't exactly shoot content the way I normally would in my own space. And in the run-up to a work trip abroad, I would kill myself in the kitchen at home, trying to bank enough recipes to post while I was away. I hardly ever made enough and would often have to hit the ground running as soon as I got home just to get back in the mix. However, in October 2022, I made a promise to myself to start really focusing on Instagram and trying to make it happen. As much as I loved my job as a personal chef, the lifestyle was becoming increasingly unsustainable. I hardly ever saw my friends and family and my body clock was always messed up with all the different time zones. I would often wake up in the middle of the night with no idea where I was, totally disoriented. A real turning point was when I woke up in the night next to Cameron and freaked out for a moment that I had sleepwalked into bed with a client! These occurrences, paired with a few other ordeals like hormone imbalances and problems with my health, made it abundantly clear that a change had to happen. My periods were completely irregular, I was suffering from terrible acne, and my eating habits had begun to affect my mental health. It felt as though I was constantly on the brink of a meltdown. I had to explore other options.

I took on a full-time role as a personal chef for just one client in the UK. This meant I could stay in one time zone and have more time to do the things I had been missing out on, as well as focus on growing my socials. I promised to stick to a posting schedule of three times a week, on a Sunday, Tuesday, and Thursday, to really try and make Instagram take off. I haven't missed a day and I think that has definitely played a role in my success on the app. Unfortunately, my new client was not a good match and I became even busier than I had been before, so I eventually resigned from that role and took the plunge into pursuing Instagram full time. Up to that point I hadn't made a penny from the app, but I knew it was going in the right direction and very luckily it all worked out. Now I work mostly as a recipe creator online, but I still do the occasional dinner party or event—just to keep my inner chef happy!

Having a community on Instagram has brought me nothing but joy. If you have ever liked, commented on, or shared one of my recipes, thank you! Building relationships with people who love to re-create my recipes, as well as working alongside brands I've looked up to and admired for years, has all been a dream. Being asked to write this cookbook was—and is—possibly the biggest pinch-me moment of my life! I am so excited to have written it and hope that it brings joy, happiness, and nourishment to your kitchen. Through working as a personal chef, I've learned how to create delicious, beautiful, healthy meals with just a few ingredients and little time, so now I want to share what I have learned with you. I want to show you the tips and tricks that make it possible to turn just a few unprocessed ingredients into something hearty and satisfying, no matter how much time you have to play with.

A NOTE ON INGREDIENTS

My style of cooking focuses on simplicity—I mostly use just a handful of ingredients but always try to ensure they are of the highest quality. This stems from the Italian influence on my cooking style but also from the countless times I have had little available to work with when having to prepare meals for clients. I am also a huge advocate for sourcing ingredients that are more environmentally sustainable. I am aware that this is not always feasible from an economic point of view but even just doing little bits here and there where you can is better than nothing.

Up until recently I followed a plant-based diet, although my cooking has always been customizable to suit all dietary requirements. I got into plant-based eating primarily for health reasons; however, as the years passed it began to feel too restrictive and was starting to take away my enjoyment around food. I have since learned that following a balanced diet works best for me to be in optimal health, both mental and physical. Although I am hugely in favor of the plant-based diet and will always encourage people to eat more plants, as is my aim with this book, adopting a "one diet fits all" mentality can be unhelpful. We are all different and have different needs, and diet can be much more nuanced than one might think. Ultimately, I believe listening to your body is very important for living a happy, healthy life. The addition of animal protein would not be unusual in some of the recipes you will find here, but they are also perfectly delicious without. It was important to me for this book to appeal to all diets, which is why it is plant-forward with suggestions of alternatives—that way nobody gets left out!

To make the book as inclusive as possible, when it comes to animal products, I've tested them all with vegan and non-vegan ingredients but leave it up to you to use your milk, cream, butter, cheese, chicken, etc., of choice (there are alternatives for everything these days). I hope this means you can tailor the recipes exactly to your taste. I've also flagged which recipes are naturally gluten free (GF) or that have a gluten-free option (GFO).

Having a pantry in your kitchen stocked with long-lasting, jarred items like kimchi and gochujang and an arsenal of condiments like soy sauce and rice wine vinegar means you will never be far from a quick, delicious meal—even if the vegetable compartment of your fridge is lacking. Some of these might not be familiar but can be found in the world foods section of most major supermarkets and are really useful staples to have on hand. It also means that when you are tired and short on time you will be much less likely to turn to ultra-processed options, which are everywhere and often marketed as the "quick and easy" option when it comes to following a plant-based diet.

Listed opposite are some of the ingredients you will always find stocked in my fridge or pantry. These allow me to have quick lightbulb ideas when I'm feeling lazy or just at a loss for what to make. I'm a big carbohydrate lover and, as you probably already know, a good balanced meal consists of protein, fats, carbohydrates, and fiber. I often start by looking at the carbohydrates I have available, and then I consider my mood. Do I want pasta, rice, or potatoes? Once I have that down, I think about flavor combinations I usually enjoy with these. That's when I scour the pantry or fridge door for sauces and condiments that I know I can use. Lastly, I decide on vegetables. Most of the time, I just use what's available in the fridge. We've all heard about how important it is to "eat the rainbow," and don't get me wrong, I love eating all the colors. But when you've had a long day and you just want to eat and go to bed, don't let the pressure get to you! As long as you're eating a couple of colors at each meal and making sure you've got lots of variety over the week, it's important to cook and eat what makes you feel good. If that means eating a bowl of pasta with only one vegetable for dinner, go for it. Life is about balance!

Having most of the below stocked will help you whip up the recipes in this book.

Beans

Capers

Cashews

Chipotle paste

Coconut milk

Gochujang

Harissa paste

Kimchi

Lentils

Mustards: *Dijon, whole-grain, English*

Nutritional yeast

Oils: *olive oil, sesame oil, crispy chile oil*

Pasta

Pickles

Ponzu

Quinoa

Rice

Roasted peppers *(in a jar)*

Sauerkraut

Shawarma paste or marinade

Soy sauce

Spices: *ground turmeric, ground cumin, ground coriander, paprika, garam masala, fenugreek leaves*

Sun-dried tomatoes

Tahini

Vinegars: *white wine, sherry, red wine, rice wine, balsamic*

I hope that this book not only saves you time in the kitchen and makes for more relaxed, nourishing, and comforting mealtimes but also gives you inspiration and a love for ingredients and cooking. It can be such a relaxing and therapeutic activity; spending more time in the kitchen can give you space to unwind and find joy in the process. Whether you have 15 minutes or a whole afternoon, there is something in here for you. You deserve it.

15 MINUTES OR LESS

There is quite a common misconception that as a chef you eat well. While this has some truth to it in that you are often tasting things as you go, the reality is that when you come home from a long day of work, you often end up eating toast with butter over the sink. We all know what it's like to reach the end of the day and have no energy left to stand in the kitchen for an hour. This first chapter is designed for those moments. It is a collection of some favorite recipes from my roster of emergency dinners, when you are in dire need of nutrients and goodness but don't have the energy to stand up for longer than 15 minutes.

STICKY "CHICKEN" SKEWERS

These skewers are so delicious and easy to prepare that I bet no one would guess it took you just 15 minutes to make them! You can serve them either as a side along with other Asian-inspired dishes (perhaps the Zingy Cucumber and Tahini Salad on page 203) or simply with rice, noodles, or salad for a perfect weeknight dinner.

Mix the soy sauces, garlic, ginger, sesame oil, rice wine vinegar, honey, and lime juice in a bowl and then stir in the chicken pieces. Let this marinate for 5 minutes while you prep the rest of the ingredients.

Skewer the chicken pieces on to metal skewers about 9½ inches / 24cm long; soak wooden ones in water for 15 minutes before using to prevent them from burning. (Alternatively, you could just cook the chicken pieces.) Heat the vegetable oil in a frying pan and fry the skewers over high heat for about 4 minutes on each side. Once the chicken is caramelized around the edges, spoon any remaining marinade over the top and cook for 2 minutes.

Heat the precooked rice (or noodles) following the instructions on the package. Put the skewers on a plate, serve with the rice or noodles, and top with the reduced marinade from the pan, the green onions, chile, and crispy fried onions. Finish with a squeeze of lime juice.

TIP: To make this gluten free use GF soy sauce and make sure the crispy fried onions are GF.

SERVES 2 — GFO

2 tbsp light soy sauce

2 tbsp dark soy sauce (or use another 2 tbsp of light soy if you don't have it)

1 garlic clove, crushed to a paste

1-inch / 2.5cm piece of ginger, finely grated

1 tbsp sesame oil

1 tbsp rice wine vinegar

1½ tbsp honey

Squeeze of lime juice, to taste

10½ oz / 300g plant-based chicken pieces (or raw chicken breast)

1 tsp vegetable oil

TO SERVE

7 oz / 200g package of precooked rice (or noodles)

2 green onions, thinly sliced

1 red chile, sliced or diced

2 tbsp crispy fried onions

Juice of ½ lime

SPEEDY SUN-DRIED TOMATO PASTA

This is something that was born out of pure desperation. I came home late after a very long, hard shift at work and had a visceral craving for pasta. We were going away the following morning, so the fridge was empty, save half a jar of sun-dried tomatoes. It has been a frequent dinner choice ever since. I also found it to be a big hit with the children of my clients—a true crowd-pleaser.

Put all the sauce ingredients into a food processor and blend until smooth, adding a splash of water if needed, and then warm up gently in a saucepan large enough to house all the pasta. Do not let it boil.

Meanwhile, cook the pasta in a saucepan of salted, boiling water until al dente, usually 8 to 12 minutes, depending on the shape.

Drain the pasta, reserving some of the cooking water. Stir the pasta into the sauce and add some of the cooking water to loosen it to your desired consistency. (I would always make it slightly saucier as it tends to dry quite quickly.)

Serve with plenty of black pepper and basil leaves.

TIP: To make this gluten free use GF pasta and to make it vegan use nutritional yeast instead of parmesan. For a nut-free option swap the cashews for white beans or tofu.

SERVES 2 — GFO

7oz / 200g mafaldine pasta (or linguine, penne, fusilli, spaghetti)

Black pepper

Basil leaves, to serve

FOR THE SAUCE

5 to 6 sun-dried tomatoes, plus 1 tbsp of their soaking oil

Handful of cashews

1 tbsp freshly grated parmesan or nutritional yeast

1 tbsp tomato paste

1¼ cups / 300ml vegetable stock

24

FRITTATENSUPPE

This is an Austrian classic. It translates as "pancake soup" and may sound odd, but it is such a comforting, delicious recipe and used to be a staple in my diet when living in Vienna. We had easy access to the mountains and so would often go skiing in the winter months; I have very fond memories of slurping on a big bowl of frittatensuppe in wooden huts halfway down the mountains so this recipe is very special to me. You can either buy a good-quality beef or vegetable consommé or broth or make your own—prepare it in advance and keep it in the freezer to ensure this recipe remains under 15 minutes!

If making the broth from scratch, heat the oil in a large saucepan and then sauté the onions over medium-low heat until starting to color; this should take about 5 minutes. Add all the remaining veg, herbs (except the chives), peppercorns, and a pinch of salt and sauté for 10 minutes before topping up with the water. Bring to a boil, making sure any bits stuck to the bottom are scraped up to ensure maximum flavor. Lower the heat and let it simmer with a lid on for 30 to 45 minutes, keeping an eye on it to ensure that it doesn't bubble over.

Season to taste and then strain out the vegetables to create a clear consommé. Set aside while you make the pancakes.

Put the flour and salt into a bowl, pour in the milk, and mix together until you have a smooth batter. Heat the oil in a large frying pan over medium heat and ladle in some of the mixture. Swirl it to the edges of the pan and cook for 3 minutes on one side, then flip over and cook for 2 minutes on the other. Slide the pancake onto a plate and repeat the process, adding more oil as needed, until all the batter has been used up. Layer the pancakes on top of each other and then roll up into a sausage shape and slice into ½-inch / 1cm strips.

Heat up the broth or consommé, ladle into bowls, and then drop in a handful of the sliced pancakes. Top with the chopped chives.

SERVES 3 TO 4 — GFO

FOR THE BROTH
(OR USE 2 CUPS /
480ML BEEF
OR VEGETABLE
CONSOMMÉ)

1 tbsp olive oil

2 white onions,
roughly chopped

2 carrots, roughly chopped

2 celery stalks,
roughly chopped

1 leek, roughly chopped

3 to 4 garlic cloves, crushed
to a paste

4 to 5 sprigs of thyme

4 to 5 sprigs of parsley

3 to 4 bay leaves

1 tsp black peppercorns

Salt, to taste

2 quarts / 2 liters water

¼ cup / 10g chopped chives,
to serve

FOR THE PANCAKES

⅔ cup / 80g all-purpose
flour

Pinch of salt

1 cup / 240ml milk of choice

1 tsp sunflower oil plus
more as needed

TIP: Once cool, the remaining broth will keep in the fridge for up to 1 week or can be frozen for up to 3 months. Make sure you use a gluten-free flour to make this suitable for those with allergies.

CREAMY LEMON PASTA

This simple dish of pasta and peas, often served to me at friends' houses when I was young, fills me to the brim with childhood comfort and nostalgia. I've slightly elevated it here by adding copious amounts of garlic and lemon. Throw in a fancy pasta shape and it looks like you've made a real effort!

Cook the pasta in a saucepan of boiling water according to the instructions on the package.

Heat the olive oil in a large frying pan (big enough to hold all the cooked pasta) and sauté the shallot over medium heat for 5 minutes, then add the garlic and cook for 1 minute.

Pour in the cream to deglaze the pan (this just means releasing the flavor that's stuck to the bottom of the pan with liquid), then add the stock cube and peas. Stir well so that the stock cube becomes thoroughly amalgamated and the peas cook through.

Drain the pasta, reserving some of the cooking water, then add the cooked pasta and a splash of the cooking water to the pan along with the lemon zest and a big squeeze of lemon juice. Mix well, season with salt and pepper, and serve immediately.

TIP: Keep it child-friendly by decreasing the lemon juice and zest, or just serving it on the side. To make this gluten free simply use GF pasta.

SERVES 2 — GFO

7oz / 200g mafalda corta pasta (or fusilli, shells, penne)

1 tbsp olive oil

½ shallot, diced

5 garlic cloves, finely chopped or grated

¾ cup plus 2 tbsp / 200ml heavy cream of choice

¼ vegetable stock cube

⅔ cup / 100g frozen peas

Zest and juice of ½ lemon

Salt and black pepper

29

KIMCHI NOODLE STIR-FRY

Recipes like this make me very happy. They tend to be the result of a fridge raid when supplies are low. This was born from needing dinner the night before going away for a week, when no fresh vegetables were available except for some dodgy-looking green onions that, once trimmed, were just about usable. The half jar of kimchi in the fridge and lone pack of dried noodles in the pantry became best friends. Depending on the jar of kimchi, these can either be mild or very spicy, so choose wisely!

First, bring a saucepan of water to a boil for your noodles.

Drain the kimchi, being sure to catch all the juice in a bowl. Add the soy sauce, rice vinegar, sugar, and gochujang to the kimchi juice and mix well. Pour into a saucepan and bring to a boil, then turn down to a simmer.

When the water has reached a boil, cook the noodles according to the package instructions (2 to 3 minutes for fresh and 8 to 10 for dried noodles). While they are boiling, roughly chop the kimchi. Once the noodles are cooked, drain well and add them to the sauce along with the chopped kimchi.

Mix well, scatter the sliced green onions and sesame seeds over the top, and serve hot!

TIP: To make this gluten free make sure you use GF soy sauce and gochujang, and rice noodles (the size and shape are up to you) instead of udon noodles. Sriracha sauce is also a welcome addition if you like more heat.

SERVES 2 — GFO

2 nests (85g) fresh or dried udon noodles

1⅓ cups / 200g kimchi

1 tsp soy sauce

1 tsp rice wine vinegar (or use lemon/lime juice)

1 tsp sugar

1 tsp gochujang

Handful of sliced green onions

1 tbsp sesame seeds

CAVOLO NERO GNOCCHI

Having a package of gnocchi on standby in your pantry is an absolute must, always. If you are someone who has little time and motivation to cook, these little potatoey pillows of joy will be your saving grace. This recipe can be modified to suit the season or just what you have at home in the fridge. You can swap the cavolo nero, also known as lacinato kale, for spinach, curly kale, or even the sun-dried tomato sauce from the recipe on page 24.

Fill a large saucepan with 2 quarts / 2 liters of water, season with a generous pinch of salt, and bring to a boil. Add the cavolo nero, stems and all, and cook for 1 minute. Carefully remove with a sieve, tongs, or spider and transfer to a high-speed blender (or blitz it in a large bowl with an immersion blender). Add the beans, along with the liquid from the can, and squeeze in the lemon juice. Season well, then blend until smooth.

Bring the same pan of water back to a boil, then add the gnocchi and cook for 2 to 3 minutes, or until each piece is floating. Drain and set aside.

Heat the olive oil in a large frying pan over medium heat, add the garlic and half the sliced chile, and fry for 1 minute, then add the gnocchi and sauté until golden. Pour in the sauce and let it simmer for a couple of minutes.

Serve up in wide bowls and top with the mozzarella, lemon zest, remaining sliced chile, a drizzle of olive oil, and plenty of cracked black pepper.

TIP: To make this gluten free use GF gnocchi.

SERVES 2 TO 3 — GFO

3½ oz / 100g cavolo nero (lacinato kale), roughly chopped (1½ cups)

1 x 15-oz / 425g can cannellini beans (or any white beans)

Juice of 1 lemon and the zest of ½

1 x 16-oz / 454g package of gnocchi

2 tbsp olive oil, plus a drizzle to serve

2 garlic cloves, thinly sliced

2 red chiles, thinly sliced

Salt and black pepper

Handful of shredded mozzarella, to serve

WARM MUSTARDY CHICKEN, SLAW, AND SAUERKRAUT SANDWICH

This is without a doubt the best sandwich that has ever passed my lips. If you aren't a fan of very strong, salty flavors, then this, perhaps, is not for you. But if, like me, you love anything with a bit of punch, proceed with joy!

Begin by shredding the plant-based or real cooked chicken into smaller pieces. Heat the olive oil in a frying pan and lightly fry the chicken for 3 to 4 minutes to warm it through.

In a bowl, mix together the mustard and mayo and season to taste. In a separate bowl, add 1 tablespoon of the mustard-mayo to the sliced cabbage to make a slaw. Add the chicken to the remaining sauce in the bowl and mix well.

Layer up the sandwich starting with the sliced pickle, then chicken, cabbage, and kraut on top. Enjoy!

TIP: To make this gluten free use GF bread.

SERVES 1 — GFO

2¼ oz / 60g cooked plant-based chicken or cooked chicken pieces

1 tsp olive oil

1½ tbsp whole-grain mustard

2 tbsp mayo of choice

Handful of shredded red cabbage

2 slices of your favorite sandwich bread

1 large pickle, sliced

2 tbsp sauerkraut

Salt and black pepper

SPICY CORN CHOWDER

This little spicy number is a great way to get your sinuses cleared! It's sweet and creamy but with a spicy kick—perfect on a cold day. I always have a big bag of corn skulking in the back of my freezer so that I can whip this up at any time.

Bring the stock to a boil in a large saucepan, add the corn, and simmer for 5 minutes. Remove a couple large spoonfuls of corn, dry off, and fry in a hot pan with 1 teaspoon of the olive oil until charred.

Meanwhile, heat the remaining 1 tbsp olive oil in a frying pan and fry the onion until just starting to color, then add the garlic, ginger, and chile. Fry for 1 minute more and then add it to the pan of corn and stock.

Pour in almost all the coconut cream, reserving some to serve, and use an immersion blender to blitz until roughly smooth.

Ladle into bowls and swirl in the remaining coconut cream. Top with the charred corn, fresh cilantro, lime wedges for squeezing over, and more chile, if desired.

SERVES 2 TO 3 — GF

1⅔ cups / 400ml vegetable stock

Scant 4 cups / 500g frozen corn kernels

1 tbsp plus 1 tsp olive oil

½ white onion, roughly chopped

4 garlic cloves, roughly chopped

2-inch / 5cm piece of ginger, roughly chopped

1 red chile, diced, plus extra to serve (optional)

¾ cup plus 2 tbsp / 200ml coconut cream or full-fat coconut milk

TO SERVE

Fresh cilantro

Lime wedges

SUMMER ROLLS WITH SPICY PEANUT DRESSING

It's not often we get scorching-hot days in the UK but when we do, this is the kind of recipe I crave. It's no-cook and comes together so quickly. It's also one of my favorite things to eat when I want something fresh, crunchy, and nutritious that's not a salad. This one is great because you can use whatever veg you have available and any protein you want—I tend to use tofu but cooked shrimp or chicken work just as well. It's the perfect light but nourishing lunch and the textures are perfection!

Whisk together all the dipping sauce ingredients (except the sesame seeds) in a bowl, adding a little water to create a dipping consistency. Taste and adjust the seasoning, then transfer to a bowl and sprinkle with the sesame seeds.

Submerge one of the rice paper wraps in a big bowl of warm water for 10 to 20 seconds to soften and then place on a board. Put a pinch of each of the veggies, a few tofu strips, and a couple of mint leaves about ¾ inch / 2cm from the bottom of the wrapper and then roll up, folding in the sides as you go along. Continue until you've made them all.

Serve immediately (they get very sticky!) with the dipping sauce alongside.

TIP: Omit the sriracha if you don't like it spicy. And use GF soy sauce to make it gluten free.

SERVES 2 (CAN EASILY BE SCALED UP) — GFO

8 to 10 Vietnamese rice paper wraps

1 carrot (3 oz / 80g), peeled and cut into matchsticks

2 handfuls of finely shredded red cabbage

½ cucumber (3 oz / 80g), cut into matchsticks

2 green onions, thinly sliced lengthwise

1 red chile, seeded and cut into matchsticks

3 oz / 80g firm tofu, cut into matchsticks

Small handful of mint leaves

FOR THE PEANUT DIPPING SAUCE

3 tbsp smooth natural peanut butter

¼ cup / 60 ml toasted sesame oil

1 tbsp sriracha

1 tbsp sushi vinegar or rice wine vinegar

1 tbsp soy sauce

½ tsp honey, or to taste

Juice of 1 lime

1 tbsp sesame seeds

BASIL, ZUCCHINI, AND PISTACHIO PASTA

Fresh herbs are a wonderful way to jazz up any dish and make it special. Here they come together to make a pesto-type sauce that's bursting with flavor. The pistachios provide a delicious sweetness and crunch and the lemon elevates each bite.

Bring a large saucepan of salted water to a boil and cook your pasta according to the package instructions.

Heat 1 tablespoon of the olive oil in a large frying pan (big enough to hold the cooked pasta) and fry the zucchini rounds until golden brown.

Bash up the pistachios in a large mortar and pestle and then remove them. Do the same with the garlic, along with a pinch of salt, until it turns into a paste, and then add all the herbs and bash together with the garlic. If you have enough space, continue bashing and grinding and then add the pistachios back in with the rest of the olive oil. If you don't have space in your mortar, tip the herbs, garlic paste, and pistachios into a bowl and mix well with the oil.

Once the pasta is cooked, drain it, reserving some of the cooking water. Add the pasta to the pan of zucchini, followed by the herby paste and a splash of the pasta water. Mix so that the paste coats the pasta, and finish with a big squeeze of lemon juice!

TIP: Use GF pasta to make this gluten free.

SERVES 2 — GFO

7 oz / 200g mafaldine pasta (or linguine, pappardelle, spaghetti)

3 tbsp olive oil

1 large zucchini, sliced into ¼-inch / 0.5cm rounds

Handful of pistachios, shelled

1 garlic clove

Big handful of fresh mint, chopped

Big handful of fresh basil, chopped

Big handful of fresh parsley, chopped

Lemon juice, to taste

Salt and black pepper

30 MINUTES OR LESS

This chapter will show you that just 30 minutes can be golden in the kitchen. It gives you enough time to play with a couple more vegetables or use the oven to give you more flavor for less work. It's the perfect amount of time to throw something together after work, or during a lunch break if you work from home. The key is just having the right ingredients stocked. Check out my list of key ingredients on page 19 so that you are ready for seamless, delicious mealtimes.

RAINBOW SLAW
NOODLE SALAD

A good salad, in my opinion, requires a decent amount of tang and crunch. This salad fulfills both of those necessities and more. You can mix it up and use whatever veg you have available, but I would strongly recommend using cabbage, as it really is the star of the show when it comes to texture. If you have a mandoline, you could easily cut the prep time in half—just watch your fingers!

Start by combining the dressing ingredients in a small bowl, loosening with water at the end to create a thick but saucy consistency.

Boil your rice noodles according to the instructions on the package, then drain and rinse in cold water until totally cool. Squeeze out any excess water and set aside on a few sheets of paper towels while you prepare the rest.

Slice the veg into thin matchsticks, put them into a bowl with the noodles and pour the dressing over the top. Mix well and let infuse while you sauté the tofu.

Heat some sesame oil in a frying pan and lightly fry the tofu until golden. Divide the noodles between two bowls and top with the tofu and sliced avocado. Scatter with chopped green onions and sesame seeds and serve with wedges of lime for squeezing on top.

TIP: This salad stays crunchy for 2 days even after adding the dressing, so if you double up the quantities it will make delicious leftovers!

SERVES 2 — GF

3 nests (85g) rice noodles

¼ red cabbage

¼ napa or green cabbage

2 bell peppers

1 large carrot

Drizzle of sesame oil

7 oz / 200g firm tofu, cut into bite-size chunks

½ avocado, sliced

FOR THE DRESSING

1 heaped tbsp white miso paste

3 tbsp sesame oil

1 tbsp rice wine vinegar

1 tbsp honey (or sweetener of choice)

Juice of ½ lemon

TO SERVE

Chopped green onions

Sesame seeds

Lime wedges

SUPER-QUICK CAESAR-ESQUE SALAD

This is easily my all-time favorite salad. It's creamy, tangy, crunchy, and perfect for a quick lunch or dinner on a summer's day. I'm a huge advocate of an unprocessed diet, but on the odd occasion I like to indulge in a plant-based "chicken" tender, especially for this recipe! If you have an air fryer, this will take you no time at all, but the oven will do just as well. Using breaded tenders or goujons adds such a welcome crunch, but using plain cooked chicken breast or plant-based alternatives works nicely too.

If using an oven, preheat it to 375°F.

Drizzle the bread with the olive oil, sprinkle with the oregano and onion and garlic granules, and roast for 15 to 20 minutes (or air fry for 5 to 7 minutes, until crispy). Roast the tenders according to the instructions on the package.

Put all the dressing ingredients into a blender and add just a splash of water to begin with. Whiz until smooth, adding more water bit by bit until you get a good, thick but pourable consistency.

Rinse and dry the romaine lettuce and chop into chunky pieces. Put them into a large bowl. Chop the chicken tenders into bite-size pieces and add them to the bowl along with the toasted bread cubes. Pour in the dressing, mix well, and serve immediately.

TIP: Serving with parmesan also adds a nice salty flavor if you're not exclusively plant-based. And, of course, use GF bread to make it gluten free.

SERVES 2 — GFO

1 large slice of bread, cubed

1 tsp olive oil

½ tsp dried oregano

½ tsp onion granules

½ tsp garlic granules

4 to 5 chicken tenders of choice

1 to 2 heads of romaine lettuce

FOR THE DRESSING

2 handfuls of cashews

1 tbsp capers

1 tsp Dijon mustard

1 tsp honey (or sweetener of choice)

1 tsp white wine vinegar

Salt and black pepper

SHAWARMA MUSHROOM FLATBREADS

There are a few things I always have lurking in my cupboards to help me get maximum flavor with minimal effort, and a good shawarma paste is one of them. It hardly needs any accessories and works as a marinade on most things with just an extra lick of olive oil and a good pinch of salt. It's also one of those things that seems to last forever in the fridge once opened.

Start by combining 1 tablespoon of the olive oil and the shawarma paste in a bowl. Tear the mushrooms and add them to the bowl, season with a good pinch of salt, then coat them in the paste so that the flavors infuse. Set aside while you prep the pickled onion.

Put the onion into a small bowl along with the lemon juice and a big pinch of salt, then give it a rough mix and allow to sit for a couple of minutes, until light pink and juicy.

In another bowl, mix the yogurt and tahini and season with salt.

To make the slaw, mix all the ingredients together with a good pinch of salt and set aside.

Heat the remaining 1 tablespoon olive oil in a frying pan over high heat and fry the marinated mushrooms for about 10 minutes, until charred and caramelized.

Warm the flatbreads in a separate dry pan or straight on a flame if you have a gas stovetop (be careful and use tongs). Let them sit for about 30 seconds per side and keep flipping until they feel warm to the touch—this goes for both pan or direct flame. Layer on the yogurt, slaw, pickled onion, and mushrooms, and finish with the pickle and parsley.

TIP: Pour olive oil into the jar of shawarma paste once it's been opened to cover the surface and prevent mold growth. If you can't find shawarma paste, you can substitute it for a premade shawarma marinade and leave out the extra oil.

SERVES 2

2 tbsp olive oil

2 tbsp shawarma paste

14 oz / 400g oyster mushrooms

2 flatbreads

1 pickle, sliced

Small bunch of parsley, chopped

Salt

FOR THE PICKLED RED ONION

½ red onion, sliced into half-moons

Juice of ½ lemon

FOR THE TAHINI YOGURT

5 tbsp / 75g plain yogurt of choice

1 tbsp tahini

FOR THE SLAW

¼ red cabbage, thinly sliced

1 tbsp vegan garlic mayo (or egg-based alternative)

Juice of ½ lemon

53

CHUNKY CANNELLINI AND TOMATO SOUP

Beans, broth, kale, and carrots—simple ingredients for a simply delicious soup. I feel like there is nothing more wholesome than a chunky, hearty soup served with crusty bread. I love this recipe because it requires little forward planning; we almost always have all the ingredients at home and it comes together very quickly, so it often makes an appearance during the winter months. It's a wonderfully simple recipe and will warm your soul in more ways than one.

Heat the olive oil in a large saucepan over medium heat, add the onion, garlic, rosemary, red pepper flakes, carrots, and tomatoes and season well with salt and pepper. Fry for 7 to 10 minutes, until soft, stirring often.

Add the cannellini beans and the liquid from the can, then pour in the stock. Bring to a boil and then let it simmer for about 10 minutes with the lid on.

Take the lid off and season to taste. Add the kale and let it wilt for 2 to 3 minutes. Finally, stir in the nutritional yeast and ladle into bowls. If you are using parmesan instead of nutritional yeast, sprinkle this over the top at the end.

Serve with crusty bread and plenty of butter (or vegan alternative).

SERVES 2 TO 3 — GF

1 tbsp olive oil

1 white onion, finely diced

4 garlic cloves, finely chopped or grated

1 sprig of rosemary

½ tbsp red pepper flakes (or to taste)

3 carrots (6⅓ oz / 180g), peeled and diced

4 large tomatoes (Roma are amazing if you can get them), diced

1 x 15-oz / 425g can cannellini beans

1 quart / 1 liter hot vegetable stock

2½ oz / 70g cavolo nero (lacinato) or curly kale, finely shredded

2 tbsp / 15g nutritional yeast or freshly grated parmesan

Salt and black pepper

TRUFFLED WHITE BEANS AND WILD MUSHROOMS

Beans are a bit of a love language for me. They are such an underrated ingredient and can be transformed into so many glorious dishes like risottos, stews, and salads. Using the oyster variety makes for delicious meaty chunks. If you have access to some real truffles, then shave away, but using truffle oil, which is much more budget-friendly, works just as well.

Preheat the oven to 400°F.

Tear up your mushrooms into a bowl and douse them in the balsamic vinegar, 2 tablespoons of the olive oil, and a pinch of salt. Allow them to marinate while the oven reaches temperature. Transfer to a baking sheet lined with parchment paper and roast until crispy, 25 to 30 minutes.

Meanwhile, heat the remaining 1 tablespoon olive oil in a large pan and fry the shallot for 5 minutes, until translucent and beginning to brown, then add the garlic and fry for 1 minute more.

Pour the white wine into the pan and let it bubble up for a couple of minutes before adding the beans and stock cube. Season well with salt and pepper, bring to a boil, and gently simmer until thick, about 20 minutes.

Stir in the nutritional yeast (or parmesan) and top with your crispy mushrooms, chives, and as much truffle oil as your heart desires!

TIP: A good hunk of sourdough alongside this is pure heaven.

SERVES 2 — GF

1 lb 2 oz / 500g oyster mushrooms

2 to 3 tbsp balsamic vinegar

3 tbsp olive oil

1 shallot, finely diced

5 garlic cloves, crushed to a paste

¾ cup / 180ml dry white wine

2 x 15-oz / 425g cans cannellini beans, drained and rinsed

1 vegetable stock cube

2 tbsp nutritional yeast or freshly grated parmesan

2 tbsp chopped chives

Truffle oil

Salt and black pepper

CREAMY MIXED MUSHROOM FARFALLE

You could use any mushrooms you like in this. I tend to lean toward brown button and portobello, which are quite easy to get your hands on. This recipe is so craveable and silky, but whenever you are using cream as the base of a sauce, I would suggest that you add a touch of vinegar to lift it from being too heavy and rich. The balsamic vinegar here gives the dish a lovely combination of sweet and tangy that cuts perfectly through the creamy sauce to balance it.

Heat a good glug of olive oil in a frying pan large enough to house all the cooked pasta and sauté the shallot over medium heat for about 5 minutes. Add the mushrooms and cook for 5 minutes or so before adding the garlic. After 1 minute, stir in the balsamic and soy sauce and then drizzle in the cream.

Let it simmer for 5 minutes and then remove from the heat and set aside while you cook your pasta in plenty of boiling salted water. Drain the pasta, reserving some of the cooking water. Mix the pasta with the creamy sauce, adding a touch of cooking water to loosen it.

Stir in the chives and plenty of black pepper. Serve hot.

TIP: I have found this to be a very good recipe to introduce mushrooms to a child's diet! Also, use GF soy sauce and pasta to make this gluten free.

SERVES 2 — GFO

Olive oil, for frying

½ shallot, finely chopped

1 lb 2 oz / 500g mixed mushrooms, roughly chopped

4 garlic cloves, finely chopped or grated

1 tbsp balsamic vinegar

1 tbsp soy sauce

¾ cup / 180ml heavy cream of choice

7 oz / 200g farfalle pasta (penne or conchiglie would also work)

2 tbsp chopped chives

Salt and black pepper

59

SQUASH SOUP WITH CRISPY CHICKPEAS AND FRIED SAGE

If you even think about skipping frying the sage leaves until crisp, you'll be committing quite a serious offense. Crispy sage leaves are the perfect, most addictive topping, especially when laid upon a silky squash soup.

Preheat the oven to 400°F.

Start by preparing the crispy chickpeas. Drain the chickpeas, pat them dry with paper towels, and then spread them out in a roasting dish with the garlic and onion granules, olive oil, and a pinch of salt and pepper. Roast in the oven for 25 minutes.

Meanwhile, heat the 2 tablespoons of olive oil in a large saucepan and fry the sage leaves until crisp. Remove from the pan and set aside on some paper towels.

In the same saucepan, fry the shallots and garlic until soft. Add the cubed squash along with the stock and bring to a boil, then turn down the heat and let it simmer for 15 minutes with the lid on.

When the squash is soft enough to break up with a fork, blitz until smooth using an immersion blender (you can also transfer it to a countertop blender—just be careful as it will be hot). Keep blending until you're happy with the consistency, adding splashes of water if needed.

Season to taste and serve with the crispy sage leaves and chickpeas on top.

SERVES 3 TO 4 — GF

2 tbsp olive oil

Handful of sage leaves

2 shallots (or 1 small white onion), roughly chopped

1 garlic clove, roughly chopped

1 butternut squash, peeled, seeded, and cubed

1 quart / 1 liter vegetable stock

FOR THE CRISPY CHICKPEAS

1 x 15-oz / 425g can chickpeas

½ tsp garlic granules

½ tsp onion granules

1 tbsp olive oil

Salt and black pepper

SIMPLE CHERRY TOMATO RIGATONI

One summer, we had a rogue tomato plant shoot out of the ground without us planting it. It was so fruitful that by the end of summer we had more cherry tomatoes than we knew what to do with. As a result we had this recipe on repeat; it really couldn't be easier to make and is ideal if you need to get on with stuff while the food is cooking—you can literally leave it unattended for almost half an hour. As tomatoes are the star of this sauce, it's best to make sure you have some really good-quality ones!

Rinse your tomatoes and pop them in a lidded pan with a generous pinch of salt and the water. Put the lid on, place over medium-low heat, and just leave it for about 20 minutes, stirring occasionally. Remove the lid and cook for 10 minutes more to allow the sauce to thicken a little.

Cook the pasta according to the package instructions, then drain (reserving a ladleful of the cooking water) and stir into the sauce. Add a little of the reserved cooking water to help it get silky.

Finish with basil, plenty of cracked black pepper, and a drizzle of olive oil.

TIP: Use GF pasta to make this gluten free.

SERVES 2 — GFO

1 lb 2 oz / 500g cherry tomatoes

7 tbsp / 100ml water

7 oz / 200g rigatoni pasta

Handful of fresh basil, finely chopped

A drizzle of olive oil

Salt and black pepper

MISO MUSHROOM GNOCCHI

Although I absolutely adore a good sweet treat, I am a savory girl at heart, and this meal always satisfies all my savory dreams. The deep umami from the miso paired with the rich and meaty mushrooms and soft pillows of gnocchi is just a match made in heaven. You can use any variety of mushroom you like or have readily available, but the oyster is, in my opinion, the best.

Put a full kettle on to boil and roughly tear up the mushrooms. Throw the mushrooms into a large dry frying pan with a sprinkle of salt. Let them cook down until all their water has evaporated and they start to sear around the edges before adding a splash of olive oil.

Once the mushrooms are looking crisp and charred, remove them from the pan and set aside. Add another glug of olive oil to the pan and add the shallot. Sauté for 5 minutes, then add the garlic to the pan.

Put the gnocchi into a separate saucepan, cover with the boiling water so that there is plenty of room above for them to rise to the surface, and put over high heat.

In a small bowl, mix the miso paste with a few large spoonfuls of the gnocchi water until smooth and pour this into the pan with the shallots and garlic. Mix well and add the mushrooms and a knob of butter.

When the gnocchi begin to float to the surface, use a slotted spoon to transfer them over into the mushroom pan and mix well. You might want to add a ladle or two of the cooking water to loosen it up. Stir in your nutritional yeast (or parmesan) and a squeeze of the lemon to taste.

Serve in bowls and finish with a healthy crack of black pepper and the fresh chives.

TIP: Use GF gnocchi to make this gluten free.

SERVES 2 — GFO

9 oz / 250g oyster mushrooms (or mushrooms of choice)

Olive oil

1 shallot, diced

3 garlic cloves, finely chopped or grated

1 x 16-oz / 454g package of gnocchi

1 tsp white miso paste

Knob of butter (or vegan alternative)

1 tbsp nutritional yeast or freshly grated parmesan

Juice of ½ lemon

Salt and black pepper

1 tbsp chopped chives, to serve

CHIPOTLE MUSHROOM TACOS

Finger food always has a big place in my heart and in my experience of working with clients with young children, it's a great way to get them to try new things. Building your own taco is rather exciting even for an adult, let alone a tot (just make sure their hands are washed!) and it's a lovely communal way to enjoy a meal.

Mix the sliced onion with the juice of half the lemon and a big pinch of salt. Set aside and let marinate until light pink.

Mix the garlic with the chipotle paste, 2 tablespoons of the olive oil, and a pinch of salt in a large bowl. Tear the mushrooms into the bowl then mix into the chipotle marinade, ensuring each mushroom is covered. Set aside.

Cut the avocado in half, remove the pit, and scoop the flesh into a bowl. Mash it up with a fork before seasoning with a sprinkle of salt, pepper, and the juice from the remaining lemon half.

Heat the remaining 1 tablespoon olive oil in a frying pan and sauté the corn until charred. Set aside.

Put the frying pan back over high heat and fry half the mushrooms for 5 to 10 minutes, until caramelized around the edges. Season well and repeat with the remaining mushrooms. (You won't need more oil for this as they already have oil on them from the marinade.)

Warm the tortillas and then either layer everything up or serve in bowls for people to create their own masterpieces! Top with sour cream (or a plant-based alternative) and a few cilantro leaves and enjoy.

TIP: Use corn tortillas to make this gluten free.

SERVES 2 — GFO

½ red onion, sliced into half-moons

1 lemon

1 garlic clove, crushed to a paste

2 tsp chipotle paste

3 tbsp olive oil

14 oz / 400g oyster mushrooms

1 avocado

⅓ cup / 60g frozen or fresh corn kernels

4 tortillas

Salt and black pepper

TO SERVE

Sour cream (or plant-based crème fraîche)

Cilantro leaves

SPRING VEG CANNELLINI BEANS

I can't express how much joy this meal gives me. The combination of lemon, garlic, and chile, paired with green vegetables and herbs, sings on my taste buds like no other. This is the perfect segue from spring to summer; it's fresh and light but hearty and wholesome at the same time.

Heat the oil in a large, deep frying pan and fry the onion and zucchini with a pinch of salt for about 5 minutes over medium heat, or until just beginning to become translucent.

Add the garlic and diced chile and cook for 2 minutes more.

Pour in the cannellini beans and the liquid from the can, then add the stock cube and the frozen peas. Season to taste with salt and pepper and bring it all to a boil, then let it simmer for 5 minutes to thicken a little.

Stir in the fresh herbs, reserving some for garnish (doing this right at the end, just before serving, allows them to retain their bright green color). Squeeze in the lemon juice to taste—I like to use a whole lemon.

Finish with the lemon zest and the reserved herbs and sliced chile. Serve with crusty bread for dipping!

SERVES 2 — GF

1 tbsp olive oil

½ white onion, diced

1 zucchini, diced

4 garlic cloves, grated

1 red chile, ½ diced and ½ sliced

1 x 15-oz / 425g can cannellini beans

¼ vegetable stock cube

⅓ cup / 50g frozen peas

2 tbsp chopped basil

2 tbsp chopped chives

2 tbsp chopped mint

Juice and zest of 1 lemon

Salt and black pepper

71

1 HOUR OR LESS

This chapter is full of the most comforting, hug-in-a-bowl recipes. A lot of them are one-pot wonders and some of them require a few different elements—but all are totally worth it. Recipes like these have a great place in my heart, as nine times out of ten you can make a big batch and store in a lidded container for the following days, where the flavors will only intensify and become even better with time.

SMASHED MISO LIMA BEANS AND CRISPY SOY MUSHROOMS

This is such a crowd-pleaser and the type of dish that raises people's eyebrows in intrigue. The first time I made this for guests, they assumed it would have a Middle Eastern flavor; when the first hits of miso and sesame oil danced on their taste buds, I could see how pleasantly surprised they were. It just works so well—think of it as a plant-focused, Asian spin on meat and potatoes.

Preheat the oven to 400°F.

Roughly tear the mushrooms into a bowl, pour in the soy sauce and sesame oil, and toss to coat. Transfer to a baking sheet and roast for 25 to 30 minutes, until crisp.

Heat the olive oil in a frying pan, add the onion and garlic, and sauté over low heat until caramelized. This will take 15 to 20 minutes.

Put the onion and garlic into a food processor with the lima beans, miso paste, and milk. Blitz until very smooth.

Spread the bean purée on a plate, top with the crispy mushrooms, chives, and green onions, and finish with a drizzle of chile oil (if using). Serve with a slice of sourdough to mop it all up and enjoy!

TIP: Make this gluten free by using GF soy sauce and bread.

SERVES 2 — GFO

1 lb 5 oz / 600g mixed mushrooms

3 tbsp soy sauce

1 tsp sesame oil

1 tbsp olive oil

½ onion, roughly chopped

4 garlic cloves, roughly chopped

1 x 15-oz / 425g can lima beans, drained and rinsed

1 heaped tbsp white miso paste

3 tbsp milk of choice

1 tbsp chopped chives

Handful of chopped green onions

1 tsp chile oil (optional)

2 slices of sourdough or your favorite bread, to serve

MISO AND MIXED MUSHROOM CONGEE

I tried congee for the first time a few years ago in a small Chinese restaurant somewhere in east London. Sadly, I cannot remember the name of the restaurant, but I have not forgotten the joy that first mouthful of congee brought me. If ever I feel the symptoms of illness approaching, this is my go-to. I load it up with ginger and garlic to help me ward off any oncoming cold.

Start by roughly tearing or chopping the mushrooms. Heat the olive oil in a saucepan over medium heat and sauté the mushrooms for about 5 minutes, or until starting to caramelize. When they have a nice color, remove from the pan and set aside.

Put all the remaining congee ingredients into the same saucepan and bring to a boil, then turn down the heat and simmer with the lid on for 25 to 30 minutes, until the rice is cooked through and it's thick. Check the seasoning—the miso and vegetable stock tend to make it salty enough but always taste anyway.

Once the congee base is cooked, take out the lemongrass stalks (if using), stir in the mushrooms to reheat, and serve in a bowl with your choice of toppings.

TIP: To make this gluten free, make sure you use GF crispy fried onions.

SERVES 2 — GFO

1 lb 2 oz / 500g mixed mushrooms

1 tbsp olive oil

1 cup / 200g short-grain rice

1 tbsp white miso paste

1 tbsp lemongrass paste (or use 2 stalks of fresh lemongrass if you can't find the paste)

2-inch / 5cm piece of ginger, finely chopped or grated

3 garlic cloves, finely chopped or grated

1 quart / 1 liter vegetable stock

Salt and black pepper

FOR THE TOPPINGS

Sliced green onion

Chile oil

Sesame seeds

Crispy fried onions

HARISSA CHICKPEAS WITH SQUASH AND POMEGRANATE

Harissa is another one of those great ingredients to always have in your pantry, as it will help you get heaps of flavor with little effort. It packs such a punch that you only need a little bit to go a long way. It pairs wonderfully with vegetables such as cauliflower, sweet potato, mushrooms, eggplant, and squash, like I am using here. A tahini drizzle feels a bit non-negotiable when it comes to a dish using harissa; the creaminess perfectly complements the heat of the harissa.

Preheat the oven to 375°F.

Arrange the squash cubes on a baking sheet and drizzle with 1 tablespoon of the olive oil, season with salt, and roast for 40 minutes.

Heat the remaining 1 tablespoon olive oil in a large pan over medium heat and fry the onion until translucent, about 10 minutes.

Add the garlic, tomato paste, and harissa and cook for 1 minute or so. Pour in the chickpeas along with the chickpea water from the can, followed by the stock. Season well with salt and pepper and bring to a boil, then lower the heat and simmer for 15 minutes.

Mix together all the tahini drizzle ingredients until you have a thick dropping consistency, then drizzle this straight over the chickpeas and top with the roasted squash. Serve topped with the pomegranate seeds, parsley, and pine nuts and enjoy with some good bread!

SERVES 2 — GF

½ butternut squash (1 lb 2 oz / 500g), peeled, seeded, and cut into ¾-inch / 2cm cubes

2 tbsp olive oil

½ red onion, finely diced

3 garlic cloves, crushed to a paste

1 tbsp tomato paste

2 tsp harissa paste

1 x 15-oz / 425g can chickpeas

¾ cup plus 2 tbsp / 200ml hot vegetable stock

Salt and black pepper

FOR THE TAHINI DRIZZLE

2 tbsp tahini

Juice of ½ lemon

Pinch of salt

3 tbsp water to loosen

TO SERVE

2 tbsp pomegranate seeds

2 tbsp chopped parsley

2 tbsp toasted pine nuts

79

HERBY BEANS WITH ROASTED BROCCOLINI

The combination of the fresh and zesty flavor from lemony, herby beans paired with the umami from the charred Broccolini is enough to tickle anyone's taste buds. This dish is so easy to whip up and is always a crowd-pleaser. It's also perfect for entertaining, as you can prep the beans ahead of time and then roast the Broccolini right before serving.

Preheat the oven to 425°F.

Put the Broccolini on a baking sheet, drizzle with olive oil, season with salt and pepper, and roast for 15 to 20 minutes, until charred around the edges.

Meanwhile, mix the diced onion and garlic in a large bowl with the juice of half a lemon and some salt. Add the chopped herbs along with the cannellini beans. Pour in the 2 tablespoons of olive oil, mix well, and season with salt and pepper.

Place a griddle pan over high heat. Slice the remaining lemon in half and griddle, cut side down, until charred, to serve alongside the dish.

Pour the beans onto a plate and top with the crisped-up Broccolini and the grilled lemon. I enjoy this with a hunk of good crusty bread!

SERVES 2 — GF

9 oz / 250g Broccolini, trimmed

2 tbsp olive oil, plus extra for drizzling

½ red onion, finely diced

1 garlic clove, finely chopped or grated

1½ lemons

2 tbsp fresh chopped chives

2 tbsp fresh chopped parsley

1 tbsp fresh chopped basil

1 x 15-oz / 425g can cannellini beans, drained and rinsed

Salt and black pepper

CHARRED CAULIFLOWER
ON SESAME BEANS

This is one of those dishes that looks like an absolute showstopper but requires hardly any effort at all, plus technically it's all done in one pot, so there's very little clean-up afterward! The tahini in the beans gives such a wonderful, nutty depth of flavor and when paired with charred cauliflower it is a match made in heaven!

Preheat the oven to 400°F and line a baking sheet with parchment paper.

Heat 1 tablespoon of the olive oil in a large frying pan over high heat. While it is heating up, quarter the cauliflower and add the chunks to the pan, flat edges down, with a pinch of salt. Cook for 5 to 7 minutes on both flat sides. Once they look golden, transfer to the lined baking sheet and roast in the oven for 25 minutes.

Put the sliced red onion into a bowl, squeeze the lemon juice over the top, and add a big pinch of salt. Let rest for 5 minutes and then lightly stir with your fingers until light pink. Set aside.

Meanwhile, put another 1 tablespoon of oil into the same pan you seared the cauliflower in and fry the shallot with a pinch of salt for 5 minutes. Add the garlic and cook for 1 minute before pouring in the beans and their liquid, along with the stock. Bring to a boil and then turn down to a simmer for 5 minutes before stirring in the tahini. Add water if it looks too dry.

Top the beans with the cauliflower and serve with the pickled onion, chopped parsley, pomegranate seeds, and sesame seeds.

SERVES 4 — GF

2 tbsp olive oil

1 cauliflower

½ red onion, sliced into half-moons

Juice of ½ lemon

1 shallot, diced

4 garlic cloves, finely chopped or grated

2 x 15 oz / 425g cans cannellini beans

7 tbsp / 100ml vegetable stock

3 tbsp tahini

Salt and black pepper

TO SERVE

Handful of chopped parsley

Handful of pomegranate seeds

Sprinkle of sesame seeds

83

BLISTERED TOMATOES AND CHICKPEAS ON CREAMY POLENTA

Polenta seems to be a bit of an underdog; you don't see it get used enough but it's a wonderful ingredient because it's cheap and cheerful and a little goes a long way. It is, of course, rather plain and definitely needs a little help in the flavor department, but plenty of cheese and butter will always remedy this.

Preheat the oven to 375°F.

Lay the tomatoes, still on the vine, on a baking sheet with the roughly drained chickpeas (a little bit of liquid is welcomed) and the unpeeled garlic cloves, then drizzle with the olive oil. Gently mix it all so everything is glossy, season with salt and pepper, and pop in the oven for 15 to 20 minutes, until the tomatoes are bursting.

In a pan, bring the stock to a boil, turn the heat down to low, and pour the polenta in slowly, stirring continuously. Cook for 20 to 25 minutes, until it's soft and thick (adding more liquid if needed). Once cooked through, remove from the heat, stir in the butter and nutritional yeast (or parmesan), and season to taste.

The tomatoes and chickpeas should be done by now, so remove the garlic cloves and either discard them or squeeze them out of their skins and leave them in. Spoon the polenta onto warmed plates (so that the polenta doesn't cool down immediately), spoon the tomatoes and chickpeas over the top, and drizzle with any leftover juices from the baking sheet. Top with the basil leaves and more nutritional yeast (or parmesan).

TIP: Slice any leftover cooked polenta into fingers, roll in uncooked polenta granules, salt, and herbs, and lightly fry until golden on each side to create polenta fries!

SERVES 2 — GF

1 pint of cherry tomatoes on the vine (approx. 9½ oz / 270g)

1 x 15-oz / 425g can chickpeas, roughly drained

4 garlic cloves, unpeeled

2 tbsp olive oil

2 cups / 480ml vegetable stock

¾ cup plus 3 tbsp / 150g polenta

Big knob of butter (or vegan alternative)

3 tbsp nutritional yeast or freshly grated parmesan, plus extra to serve

Handful of fresh basil leaves

Salt and black pepper

85

SMASHED BEANS WITH CAPONATA

Caponata is a mixture of all my favorite vegetables and so spreading it on some of my favorite (mashed) beans seemed an obvious pairing. This is delicious, rich, and wholesome—serve it with some crusty sourdough and I promise it will make you very happy.

Put a large saucepan over medium heat, add the diced eggplant and a pinch of salt, and fry without any oil, tossing regularly, until nicely charred. Remove from the pan and set aside.

Heat the olive oil in the same pan and sauté the zucchini, shallot, celery, and red bell pepper. Add the garlic and chile and fry for 1 minute, then add the tomatoes, olives, capers, raisins, and stock and let it bubble for a couple of minutes before lowering the heat. Let simmer for 10 to 15 minutes, or until thickened, then stir in the charred eggplant.

For the beans, heat 1 tablespoon of the olive oil in a separate small frying pan over medium heat and fry the shallot and garlic until just browning. Tip into a food processor along with the cannellini beans, the lemon juice, and the remaining 1 tablespoon olive oil and season with salt and pepper. Blitz until roughly smooth.

Pour the smashed beans onto a plate, spread out, and then top with the caponata in the middle. Finish with the pine nuts, parsley, basil, and an extra drizzle of olive oil. And, as always, mop up with some delicious sourdough.

TIP: To make this gluten free use GF bread.

SERVES 2 — GFO

1 eggplant, cut into ½ to ¾-inch / 1 to 2cm dice

1 tbsp olive oil

1 zucchini, cut into ½ to ¾-inch / 1 to 2cm dice

1 shallot, diced

2 celery stalks, diced

1 red bell pepper, seeded and diced

4 garlic cloves, finely chopped or grated

1 red chile, diced

1 x 14-oz / 400g can chopped tomatoes

2 tbsp chopped green olives

2 tbsp capers

1 heaped tbsp raisins (trust me, they work)

¾ cup plus 2 tbsp / 200ml vegetable stock

1 tbsp toasted pine nuts

Handful of fresh parsley leaves

Handful of fresh basil leaves

Salt and black pepper

Sourdough or your bread of choice, to serve

FOR THE SMASHED BEANS

2 tbsp olive oil, plus extra
for drizzling

1 shallot, roughly chopped

3 garlic cloves,
roughly chopped

2 x 15-oz / 425g cans
cannellini beans, drained
and rinsed

Juice of ½ lemon

GOLDEN DAL

This is my ultimate comfort food. It is nearly impossible to make a small portion and I can usually feed a small army with the amount I wind up making. The flavors intensify and embolden with every day that passes, so it makes the perfect batch cook. Make a big vat of it and freeze whatever you don't eat for a rainy day.

Heat the sunflower oil in a deep heavy-bottomed pot, add the white onion, and sauté over medium-low heat for 10 minutes. Stir in the garlic, chile, ginger, and spices and cook for 1 minute, until the spices are fragrant.

Stir in the red lentils and yellow split peas, season with salt, and pour in the stock. Bring to a boil and then let simmer for 40 to 45 minutes, stirring occasionally and topping up with more liquid if needed.

Meanwhile, pickle the sliced red onion by putting it in a bowl with the lemon juice and a big pinch of salt. Let rest for 5 minutes and then lightly squeeze with your fingers until the onion is light pink. Set aside.

When the dal is cooked, finish with a big drizzle of the coconut cream. Pour into bowls and serve topped with the pickled red onion, cilantro leaves, chiles, and nigella seeds.

SERVES 4 TO 6 — GF

1 tbsp sunflower oil

½ white onion, finely diced

2 garlic cloves, crushed to a paste

1 red chile, seeded and finely diced

2-inch / 5cm piece of ginger, grated

1 tsp ground turmeric

½ tsp ground cumin

1 tsp ground coriander

¼ tsp ground fenugreek

1 tsp ground black pepper

¾ cup / 150g dry red lentils

Heaped ¾ cup / 150g dry yellow split peas

5 cups / 1.2 liters hot vegetable stock

3 tbsp coconut cream (the thick part at the top of a can of coconut milk)

Salt

TO SERVE

1 red onion, sliced into half-moons

Juice of ½ lemon

Small bunch of cilantro, stemmed

2 red chiles, thinly sliced

Sprinkle of nigella seeds or a combination of cumin and sesame seeds

SPINACH AND TOFU CURRY

When I was traveling around India in my twenties, I ate palak paneer at least twice a week. It is absolutely divine and I became slightly obsessed! During the period that I was dairy free, I had to find a way to make something similar and so this recipe was born, though you can of course use the traditional paneer instead of tofu.

Preheat the oven to 375°F.

Drain the tofu, pat dry with paper towels, and cut into ½-inch / 1cm cubes. Arrange on a baking sheet, drizzle with 2 tablespoons of the oil, and sprinkle with the turmeric, then season with salt and pepper. Give it all a good mix and bake in the oven for 25 to 30 minutes.

Put the rice in a fine-mesh sieve and give it a good rinse, then put it into a saucepan with a lid and pour in the water and add a pinch of salt. Bring it to a boil with the lid off, then lower the heat, clamp on the lid, and let it cook for 15 minutes before turning the heat off and letting it sit until the rest of the meal is ready.

Put the spinach into a large bowl and cover with boiling water, pushing it under the water with a wooden spoon so it wilts a little. Drain well and then blitz in a blender until a purée is formed.

Place a large pan over medium-high heat, put in the remaining 1 tablespoon oil, and sauté the onion until nicely browned, 5 to 7 minutes. Next, add the cumin and mustard seeds along with the ginger, garlic, and chiles and cook for 1 minute before adding the tomatoes. Season well with salt and pepper and stir often so nothing sticks to the pan and burns.

Once the tomatoes have softened, mush them up with the back of a spoon until everything in the pan resembles a thick paste. Add the spinach purée and season again with salt and pepper.

Bring to a boil and simmer for about 10 minutes to allow the flavors to infuse. Add the baked tofu cubes at the end, squeeze in some lemon juice to taste, and top with a little sliced red chile. Serve with the rice.

SERVES 4 — GF

1 x 1-lb / 454g block of firm tofu

3 tbsp olive oil

2 tsp ground turmeric

1½ cups / 300g basmati rice

2½ cups / 600ml water

1 lb / 454g baby spinach

1 large red onion, thinly sliced

2 tbsp cumin seeds

2 tbsp black mustard seeds

2-inch / 5cm piece of ginger, finely grated

4 fat garlic cloves, crushed to a paste

2 green chiles, seeded and finely chopped

3 Roma tomatoes (7 oz / 200g), finely chopped

Lemon juice, to taste

1 red chile, thinly sliced

Salt and black pepper

TIP: If you can get your hands on them, chapatis are also delicious with this instead of rice. Keep the curry in the fridge for up to 3 days or freeze for up to 4 months.

SILKY SQUASH BEANS

Squash, when roasted and broken down, becomes such a silky-smooth sauce and works perfectly with beans swimming in it. Plenty of olive oil and crispy sage leaves as well as a dollop of soft cheese on top make it so delicious you won't be able to stop eating it.

Bring a large saucepan of water to a boil and add the stock cube. Pour in the diced squash, lower the heat to medium, and let it gently boil for 10 to 15 minutes, until very soft.

Heat 2 tablespoons of the oil in a large frying pan and fry the sage leaves until crisp, then remove and set aside on paper towels to drain. In the same pan, fry the shallot in the sage-infused oil along with a pinch of salt for 5 minutes, followed by the garlic for 1 minute. Pour in the beans along with the liquid from the cans and stir.

Once the squash is very soft, lift it out of the stock with a slotted spoon and transfer to the pan with the beans. Add the knob of butter and then mix well with a fork so that the squash breaks down and melts with the butter into a silky sauce. If it needs loosening, add a little more of the stock. Let it simmer for 5 to 10 minutes.

Once it has thickened to your desired consistency (I like mine to be saucy but not watery), spoon into bowls and tear or spoon the mozzarella or soft cheese over the top. Finish with the crispy sage leaves, a healthy drizzle of olive oil, and a good grind of black pepper. As with all things, it is best served with a hunk of sourdough!

TIP: To make this gluten free use GF bread.

SERVES 2 TO 3 — GFO

1 vegetable stock cube

½ large butternut squash, peeled, seeded, and cubed (approx. 14 oz / 400g prepared weight)

2 tbsp olive oil, plus extra for drizzling

Handful of sage leaves

1 shallot, diced

3 garlic cloves, finely chopped or grated

2 x 15-oz / 425g cans cannellini beans

Knob of butter (or vegan alternative)

1 fresh mozzarella ball or 2 to 3 tbsp soft cheese (or vegan alternative)

Salt and black pepper

Sourdough bread, to serve

1 HOUR +

When you have more than an hour to play with, in my
opinion things get fun, and that is exactly what these
recipes are all about. Much as I love the functionality
of a quick recipe, spending time (when I have it) in the
kitchen is my dopamine: it brings me pure joy. There
is something so therapeutic about slowing down and
doing things for pleasure rather than necessity, and
these recipes will hopefully give you that same feeling
of joyfulness. Plan ahead, have all your ingredients ready,
get the radio or your favorite playlist on, and get lost
in the recipe. It is such a wonderful way to be present,
catch up with yourself, reduce your screen time (and
hopefully your stress levels), and really enjoy the process.
And it gets even better when you get to share your
creation afterward. They say the kitchen is the heart of
the home and I believe the food created in it is the soul.
Let it be rich, deep, and flavorful, and born out of love,
not just practicality.

EGGPLANT AND LENTIL MOUSSAKA

This reminds me of my friend Lily, who I met at university. She was (and still is) best friends with my partner, Cameron. I was invited over for dinner one evening and she cooked me an eggplant moussaka that I haven't stopped thinking about since. The creaminess of the béchamel and the sweet cinnamon are a comforting match made in heaven. This is now a winter staple in our household.

Preheat the oven to 375°F.

Lay the eggplant slices on a baking sheet, drizzle with 2 tablespoons of the oil, and season with salt. Roast for 40 minutes, flipping halfway through.

Meanwhile, rinse the lentils and put them into a saucepan with four times their volume (about 2 cups / 480ml) of water. Bring to a boil, then lower the heat and simmer with the lid on for 20 minutes, or until the lentils are just tender.

Heat the remaining 1 tablespoon oil in a large frying pan and sauté the shallot and carrot with a pinch of salt for 10 minutes. Add the garlic, tomato paste, oregano, bay leaf, and cinnamon and fry for 1 minute. Add the canned tomatoes and stock cube and, when the lentils have cooked, drain them and add them too. Bring to a boil, then turn the heat down to simmer for 5 minutes.

Start the béchamel by melting the butter in a small saucepan. Sprinkle with the flour and whisk until a paste forms, then slowly pour in the milk, while continuously whisking, to create a smooth texture. Sprinkle in the nutritional yeast (or cheese) and the nutmeg, then season with salt and pepper. Cook until thick enough to coat the back of a spoon.

Spread a layer of the lentil mixture in the bottom of a large ovenproof dish, followed by a layer of eggplant, more lentils, and then more eggplant. Finish with the béchamel, then bake in the oven for 30 minutes.

Cut into even portions and serve.

TIP: Sprinkling a bit of cheddar or parmesan on top before baking in the oven is always welcome, and you can use GF flour instead to make the béchamel gluten free.

SERVES 2 TO 3 — GFO

2 large eggplants (14 oz / 400g), cut lengthwise into ½-inch / 1cm slices

3 tbsp olive oil

½ cup / 100g dry Puy lentils

1 shallot, finely diced

1 carrot, finely diced

4 garlic cloves, crushed to a paste

1 tsp tomato paste

1 tsp dried oregano

1 bay leaf

1 tsp ground cinnamon

1 x 14-oz / 400g can chopped tomatoes

½ vegetable stock cube, crumbled

Salt and black pepper

FOR THE BÉCHAMEL

1½ tbsp butter (or vegan alternative)

3 tbsp flour

¾ cup plus 2 tbsp / 200ml milk of choice

1 tbsp nutritional yeast or grated cheddar

¼ tsp grated nutmeg

JERUSALEM ARTICHOKE RISOTTO

Jerusalem artichokes are my favorite root vegetable. You don't often see them in supermarkets so I would always keep an eye out for them at your local farmer's market. They are little nuggets of joy with a sweet, nutty flavor, definitely worth hunting down. Roasting them until charred and tender and then blitzing them up will give you the smoothest, most velvety sauce, perfect to stir into a risotto or even use as a soup! I should warn you though, they are nicknamed fartichokes for a reason, so proceed with caution!

Preheat the oven to 375°F.

Lay the artichokes on a baking sheet, drizzle them with 1 tablespoon of the olive oil, and season with salt and pepper before roasting for 30 to 35 minutes, until soft and gently charred. Allow to cool, then put into a food processor or blender with the cream, lemon juice, and 2 tablespoons of the stock and blitz until smooth. Set aside.

Bring the rest of the stock to a simmer and have this next to your risotto pan so you can ladle hot stock easily into the rice. Using hot stock means the rice releases starch and gives the risotto its characteristic creamy texture.

Heat the remaining 1 tablespoon olive oil in a large frying pan. Add the onion and fry for 5 minutes, until soft but not browned. Add the garlic and fry for 1 minute. Pour in a ladle of stock, bring to a simmer, and then stir in all the rice. Season as you go along so that the rice can absorb it as it cooks.

Once the stock has been fully absorbed, pour in another ladleful, keeping the risotto simmering all the while. Repeat this process, stirring occasionally, until the rice is plump and almost fully cooked. This will take at least 25 minutes.

Add the artichoke purée to the risotto and stir well to combine. Grate in the nutmeg and add the nutritional yeast (or parmesan). Serve with the chives and chestnuts scattered over and finish with a drizzle of truffle oil.

SERVES 3 — GF

4 to 5 big roots (10½ oz / 300g) of Jerusalem artichokes, peeled and roughly chopped

2 tbsp olive oil

7 tbsp / 100ml heavy cream of choice

Juice of ½ lemon

1 quart / 1 liter hot vegetable stock

½ white onion, finely chopped

4 garlic cloves, crushed to a paste

1½ cups / 300g arborio rice

¼ tsp grated nutmeg

2 tbsp nutritional yeast or freshly grated parmesan

Small bunch of chives, finely chopped

Big handful of roasted chestnuts, crumbled (or use toasted pine nuts)

2 tsp truffle oil

Salt and black pepper

SPICY, SMOKY BLACK BEAN BOWL

Black beans are little powerhouses of nutrition. They are packed with nutrients and antioxidants that aid gut and heart health. Their dark blue/purple hue means they are rich in polyphenols that can prevent chronic disease and they contain major anti-inflammatory properties, as well as being rich in both protein and fiber. I love making a big bowl of them and loading it up with rice or sweet potatoes, or even smearing them onto a tortilla and wrapping it up for an on-the-go meal.

Preheat your oven to 400°F.

Lay the sweet potato cubes on one baking sheet, drizzle with 1 tablespoon of the olive oil, and sprinkle with some salt. Spread the corn on a separate baking sheet and drizzle with a little oil and salt as well. Roast both sheets in the oven for 20 to 25 minutes, turning occasionally, until the sweet potato is tender and the corn is evenly charred.

Meanwhile, place a large, deep frying pan over medium heat with the remaining 1 tablespoon olive oil; when hot, sauté the onion until translucent, which should take about 5 minutes. Add the garlic, chipotle paste, and tomato paste and cook, stirring, for a couple of minutes before adding the black beans, along with the liquid from the cans. Season and gently bring to a boil, then turn down to a simmer for 15 to 20 minutes.

Pickle the sliced red onion by putting it in a bowl with the lemon juice and a big pinch of salt. Let rest for 5 minutes and then lightly squeeze with your fingers until the onion is light pink. Set aside.

Once the beans have thickened to your liking, serve with the roasted sweet potato, corn, and pickled onion on top, with your choice of toppings. I like avocado, sour cream, cilantro, and lime wedges for squeezing.

SERVES 2 TO 3 — GF

1 large sweet potato, diced

2 tbsp olive oil, plus extra for drizzling

Heaped ½ cup / 100g frozen or fresh corn kernels

1 red onion, diced

4 garlic cloves, finely chopped or grated

2 tsp chipotle paste

1 tbsp tomato paste

2 x 15-oz / 425g cans black beans

Salt and black pepper

FOR THE PICKLED RED ONION

1 red onion, sliced into half-moons

Juice of ½ lemon

TO SERVE

1 avocado, sliced

2 to 3 tbsp sour cream (or vegan sour cream)

Handful of cilantro leaves

½ lime, cut into wedges

HEALING BLACK DAL

If you have never tried a black dal before, now is definitely the time. This will comfort you in ways you have never been comforted before. The depth of flavor and creaminess are unmatched, and you will be spooning it straight out of the pan, I promise!

Put the beluga lentils into a bowl and cover with plenty of cold water. Let soak for at least 6 hours, ideally overnight, then drain and rinse.

Toast all the spices in a large dry saucepan for 1 minute or so, until they become very fragrant—be careful not to burn them! Remove from the pan and set aside.

Put the oil into the pan and sauté the onion for about 5 minutes, until it starts to color. Add the garlic, ginger, and toasted spices, sauté for 1 minute, and then add the tomato paste. Mix well until everything is combined into a paste.

Add the lentils to the pan along with the beans and the liquid from the cans. Mix well so each lentil is coated and then pour in the stock. Add the curry or bay leaves and bring to a gentle boil before decreasing the heat to low. Simmer with the lid on for 25 minutes, or until the lentils are soft.

Meanwhile, pickle the red onion by covering with the lemon juice and salt. Let rest for 5 minutes and then gently squeeze with your fingers until the onion turns light pink.

Once the lentils are soft, pour in the coconut milk, reserving a couple large spoonfuls for garnish. Simmer for 5 minutes and then serve topped with a drizzle of the coconut milk, the pickled onion, and cilantro leaves.

SERVES 4 TO 5 — GF

1⅓ cups / 250g beluga lentils

1 tsp ground turmeric

1 tsp chile powder (Kashmiri if possible)

1 tsp ground cumin

1 tsp ground coriander

1 tsp garam masala

¼ tsp ground fenugreek

½ tsp ground cinnamon

2 tbsp olive oil

1 red onion, diced

3 garlic cloves, finely chopped or grated

1-inch / 2.5cm piece of ginger, peeled and grated

¼ cup / 50g tomato paste

2 x 15-oz / 425g cans kidney beans

2 cups / 480ml vegetable stock

3 curry leaves or bay leaves

¾ cup plus 2 tbsp / 200ml full-fat coconut milk

Fresh cilantro, to serve

FOR THE PICKLED RED ONION

½ red onion, sliced into half-moons

Juice of ½ lemon

Pinch of salt

SLOW-ROASTED OYSTER MUSHROOM RAGU

Oyster mushrooms are so deliciously meaty and although this recipe would work with any mushrooms, I would highly recommend getting your hands on this specific variety—they really do surpass any other in texture. This is the kind of recipe I would make when I'm entertaining guests or just want something special on the weekend. It's a labor of love but the depth of flavor that comes from it is so worth it!

Preheat the oven to 375°F.

Tear the mushrooms up into thin slivers, place on a baking sheet and drizzle with the soy sauce, balsamic vinegar, Worcestershire sauce, 1 tablespoon of the olive oil, and a pinch of salt. Mix well and roast for 40 to 45 minutes, until charred.

Meanwhile, heat the remaining 1 tablespoon olive oil in a large saucepan and fry the shallot, celery, and carrot with a pinch of salt for 5 to 8 minutes, until softened. Follow with the garlic for 1 to 2 minutes, then pour in the canned tomatoes, fill one of the cans with water and add that too, along with the stock cube. If using whole tomatoes, crush them with a wooden spoon against the sides of the pan. Bring to a boil and then lower to a simmer until the mushrooms come out of the oven.

Stir the roasted mushrooms into the sauce, season to taste, and allow to reduce more while you cook your pasta according to the instructions on the package.

Drain the pasta, reserving some of the cooking water to loosen the mushroom sauce if necessary.

Mix the drained, cooked pasta into the sauce and season to taste before serving.

TIP: Use GF pasta, soy sauce, and Worcestershire sauce to make this gluten free.

SERVES 4 — GFO

1 lb / 450g oyster mushrooms

3 tbsp soy sauce

3 tbsp balsamic vinegar

2 tbsp Worcestershire sauce

2 tbsp olive oil

1 shallot, diced

1 celery stalk, diced

1 small carrot, diced

5 garlic cloves, finely chopped or grated

2 x 14-oz / 400g cans tomatoes (whole San Marzano are my favorite but other whole or chopped will work)

1 beef stock cube (or use chicken or vegetable stock cube)

12¼ oz / 350g pasta, such as rigatoni

Salt and black pepper

LEEK, POTATO, AND CELERY ROOT GRATIN

A gratin is such a good way to sneak in vegetables: they may be surrounded by lots of cream and cheese but you're still getting a few of your five a day! This is always a crowd-pleaser; it has a rich, velvety texture from the potato and the celery root and a lovely sweetness from the leeks. Children always seem to enjoy this one so it's a perfect way to get them eating the vegetables they might not usually eat. It's also quite fun to assemble and a great way to get them involved in the kitchen.

SERVES 4 TO 6 — GF

1 tbsp olive oil

1 tbsp butter (or vegan alternative)

2 leeks (14 oz / 400g), halved lengthwise and sliced into half-moons

1½ cups / 360ml heavy cream of choice

1¼ cups / 300ml unsweetened milk of choice

2 sprigs of rosemary, needles finely chopped

1 large bay leaf

½ tsp grated nutmeg

¼ vegetable stock cube, crumbled

1 whole celery root (1 lb 9 oz / 700g)

Juice of ½ lemon

2 large potatoes (1 lb 5 oz / 600g)

1¾ cups / 200g grated cheddar (or cheese of choice)

Salt and black pepper

Chopped green onions, to serve

Preheat the oven to 375°F.

Heat the olive oil and butter in a frying pan and fry the leeks over low heat until soft. Set aside 3 tablespoons of the cream and add the rest to the leeks along with the milk, herbs, nutmeg, and stock cube. Let this simmer very gently for 10 minutes, then remove from the heat and allow to infuse for 10 minutes.

Meanwhile, peel the celery root and cut in half, then cut into thin (⅛-inch / 3mm) slices. Drop the slices into a bowl of water with lemon juice in it to prevent them from discoloring. In a separate bowl, do the same with the potatoes.

Spoon a layer of the creamy leek mixture into the bottom of a large ovenproof dish and add a layer of the celery root on top followed by some grated cheese. Spoon over another layer of the leeks and cover with a layer of potato. Repeat this process, alternating between the celery root and potato, until everything is used up, ending with celery root or potato as the top layer.

Pour the reserved cream over the top, season with salt and pepper, and add a final sprinkling of cheese. Bake in the oven for 1 hour, until browned and bubbling. Let stand for 10 minutes, top with green onions, and serve.

TIP: I would enjoy this as a main, but it works perfectly alongside a roasted meat dish.

SMOKY BEAN CHILI

A good chili recipe should be in everyone's repertoire; there isn't a day when we don't have at least one container full of it ready to go in the freezer. It's another one of those you just cannot make in a small batch and the flavors get better and better as time passes. All it needs is a little spruce up with colorful toppings and you're good to go.

Heat 1 tablespoon of the oil in a large saucepan over medium heat and sauté the onion and bell peppers for about 5 minutes, or until soft. Add the carrot and celery and cook for 3 minutes, then add the garlic, chile, marjoram, and spices and sauté for 1 minute. Add all the beans, including the liquid from the cans—it's full of nutrients! Pour in the canned tomatoes and season to taste. Give everything a good stir, bring to a boil, and then simmer for 25 to 30 minutes, until reduced, thick and saucy. Stir occasionally and top up with water if it looks like it needs loosening.

Meanwhile, prepare your toppings. Cut both avocados in half and remove the pits. Criss-cross the flesh into chunky diamonds and spoon out into a bowl, then add salt and pepper and a squeeze of lemon juice to taste. Stir gently, so as not to mush the avocado completely.

Thinly slice the red onion into half-moons and put in a bowl with the remaining lemon juice. Gently squeeze the onion until it turns a light bright pink.

Serve the chili topped with the pink pickled onion, avocado, and fresh cilantro leaves.

SERVES 4 TO 5 — GF

1 tbsp olive oil

1 white onion, finely chopped

3 red/orange/yellow bell peppers, seeded and cut into ¾-inch / 2cm chunks

1 carrot, peeled and cut into ½-inch / 1cm chunks

1 celery stalk, chopped into ½-inch / 1cm slices

5 garlic cloves, finely chopped

1 fresh red chile, seeded and finely chopped

1 tbsp dried marjoram

2 tbsp ground cumin

1 tbsp ground cinnamon

1 tbsp smoked paprika

1 tsp cayenne pepper (omit if you don't like it spicy)

1 x 15-oz / 425g can black beans

1 x 15-oz / 425g can red kidney beans

1 x 15-oz / 425g can black-eyed peas

2 x 14-oz / 400g cans chopped tomatoes

Salt and black pepper

FOR THE TOPPINGS

2 ripe avocados

Juice of ½ lemon

½ red onion

Bunch of fresh cilantro
or parsley, stemmed

TIP: This tastes even better a few days later and makes for a
fantastic batch cook!

MUM'S LOVING LEEK
AND POTATO SOUP

It might sound like a cliché, but my mum is my superhero and her leek and potato soup heals me in more ways than I can put into words. My re-creation will never be as good as hers, but I've given it my best shot.

Heat the olive oil in a large saucepan, then add the leeks, onion, fennel seeds, nutmeg, and garlic. Put the lid on and sweat them down over low heat for 10 to 15 minutes.

Meanwhile, cut the potato in half, lay it flat side down, and cut into thin slices.

Add the sliced potato to the saucepan and cook for 5 minutes, until soft, then add the veg stock and bring to a boil. Turn down the heat and simmer for 5 minutes, then use an immersion blender to blend until silky smooth. Stir in the knob of butter.

Season to taste and serve with warm crusty bread.

SERVES 4 — GF

1 to 2 tbsp olive oil

3 leeks, roughly chopped

½ white onion,
roughly chopped

1 tsp fennel seeds

¼ tsp grated nutmeg

2 garlic cloves,
roughly chopped

1 large potato (no need
to peel)

1 quart / 1 liter vegetable
stock

Big knob of butter
(or vegan alternative)

Salt and black pepper

CHICKEN, LEEK, AND BACON PIE

My mum and the whole English side of my family are from up north in Lancashire and so it is simply in my blood to love a good pie. This is my favorite; it's creamy, smoky, and extremely easy to put together whether you are using vegan ingredients or not.

Preheat the oven to 375°F.

Put a nonstick frying pan over medium heat with 1 tablespoon of the olive oil and sauté the lardons for 5 to 10 minutes, until caramelized around the edges. Remove and set aside. Heat another 1 tablespoon of the oil in the same pan, and fry the chicken pieces for 5 to 10 minutes, until browned and just cooked through. (If you are cooking with meat, you won't need more oil for the chicken—just cook it in the fat released from the bacon.) Set aside and season well with salt and pepper.

Sauté the leek and shallots in the same pan you used for the chicken and lardons with the remaining 1 tablespoon olive oil. After about 5 minutes add the garlic and cook for 1 minute, then sprinkle with the flour. Cook, stirring, for a couple of minutes, or until no white bits remain. Pour in the milk and stir well so you have a smooth sauce. Stir in the stock cube, Dijon mustard, and nutmeg and mix well to combine. Let the mixture gently simmer for a couple of minutes to thicken, then transfer to a large pie dish or shallow baking dish and stir in the cream, chicken, and lardons.

Let sit for 15 minutes to cool down slightly before stirring in the herbs (this will help them retain their color).

Cut the pastry so that it fits your dish and then place it carefully on top, crimping the edges down. Brush it with milk and stab a cross in the middle to allow the steam to escape while baking. Bake in the oven for 25 to 30 minutes, or until golden.

SERVES 4 — GFO

2 to 3 tbsp olive oil

7 oz / 200g bacon (real or plant-based), cut into lardons

14 oz / 400g chicken pieces (real or plant-based), thinly sliced

1 medium leek (about 7 oz / 200g), thinly sliced

2 shallots, finely diced

4 garlic cloves, crushed to a paste

1 tbsp flour

1⅔ cups / 400ml milk of choice, plus extra for brushing

1 vegetable stock cube, crumbled

1 tsp Dijon mustard

¼ tsp grated nutmeg

7 tbsp / 100ml heavy cream of choice

2 tbsp chopped chives, parsley, and thyme

1 x 14 oz / 397g sheet of pre-rolled puff pastry

Salt and black pepper

TIP: Use GF flour and pre-rolled GF puff pastry to make this gluten free—you can usually find the pastry in the frozen section in big supermarkets or online.

PESTO BEANS AND ROASTED TOMS

Pesto is, again, one of those players that gives you a lot of flavor for very little work. It's so easy to dollop into a pasta, risotto, or sandwich to take it to the next level. I always prefer to make my own (see page 212) and lots of it, to store in the freezer for whenever I need an easy win in the kitchen.

Preheat the oven to 375°F.

Lay the cherry tomatoes on a roasting dish, cover with 1 tablespoon of the olive oil, and roast for 15 to 20 minutes, until just bursting.

Slice the stalks of the asparagus into ½-inch / 1cm rounds and halve the tips. Heat the remaining 1 tablespoon oil in a large saucepan and fry the rounds over medium heat for 1 minute, then add the tips and fry for another 1 minute or so, until they have softened. Remove from the pan.

Add a little more oil to the pan if it needs it and fry the shallot for 5 minutes, until just browning, then add the garlic and fry for 1 minute. Pour in the beans and their liquid and add the stock cube. Stir well.

Let it simmer and thicken up for 5 to 10 minutes.

Return the asparagus to the pan, swirl in the pesto, and squeeze in the lemon juice. Scatter the fresh mint, basil, pine nuts, and chile and top with the roasted tomatoes.

SERVES 2 TO 3 — GF

5¼ oz / 150g cherry tomatoes on the vine

2 tbsp olive oil, plus extra as needed

14 oz / 400g asparagus

½ shallot, diced

4 garlic cloves, finely chopped or grated

2 x 15-oz / 425g cans lima beans

¼ vegetable stock cube

3 tbsp pesto (store-bought or see page 212)

Juice of ½ lemon

Handful of fresh mint and basil leaves

1 tbsp pine nuts

1 red chile, seeded and diced or sliced

CRISPY EGGPLANT AND GROUND TOFU ON TAHINI YOGURT

Eggplant sometimes gets a bad rep but if you're unsure about it this recipe is here to change your mind. When roasted in the oven eggplant becomes almost crisp-like with a soft middle and a craveable flavor. It pairs perfectly with tahini and I can guarantee these Middle Eastern flavors will turn any eggplant hater into a lover!

Preheat the oven to 400°F.

Slice the eggplant crosswise into ½ to ¾-inch / 1 to 2cm disks, transfer to a plate, douse in salt so that all the pieces are covered, and let sit for 10 minutes.

Meanwhile, pickle the onion by putting it into a bowl with the lemon juice and a big pinch of salt. Let sit for 5 minutes and then lightly squeeze with your fingers until light pink. Set aside.

Wipe away the liquid that has surfaced on the eggplants. Lay them on a baking sheet, making sure you leave space between each one so that they crisp up, drizzle generously with the olive oil, season with a bit of salt and pepper, and roast in the oven for 30 minutes, flipping halfway through cooking.

Now for the ground tofu: heat the olive oil in a pan over high heat and use your hands to crumble the tofu into the pan. Add the garlic and onion granules, soy and Worcestershire sauces, and ground cumin and season with salt and pepper. Fry until crisp around the edges, usually about 15 minutes.

In a separate bowl, mix the yogurt and tahini together. Season with salt and pepper and set aside.

Spoon the yogurt mixture onto a plate and top with the roasted eggplant and crispy tofu. Scatter the pickled onion, pomegranate seeds, pistachios, and parsley over the top and serve!

TIP: The ground tofu can be subbed with ground lamb or beef if you're not vegetarian. Use GF soy and Worcestershire sauces to make this gluten free.

SERVES 2 — GFO

1 large eggplant

¼ cup / 60ml olive oil

¼ cup / 60ml plain yogurt of choice

1 heaped tbsp tahini

1 tbsp pomegranate seeds

Handful of pistachios, roughly chopped

1 tbsp chopped parsley

Salt and black pepper

FOR THE PICKLED RED ONION

½ red onion, sliced into half-moons

Juice of ½ lemon

FOR THE CRISPY GROUND TOFU

1 tbsp olive oil

6 oz / 175g firm tofu

½ tsp garlic granules

½ tsp onion granules

1 tbsp soy sauce

1 tsp Worcestershire sauce

1 tsp ground cumin

119

WILD GARLIC RISOTTO

Wild garlic is one of nature's greatest gifts! It comes into season around mid-February and is finished by the end of April. You can find it growing in shaded, sloped areas that are usually near water and you will smell it before you see it! I tend to go wild garlic foraging once or twice during a season and turn it into pestos and oils to serve me during the out-of-season months. It's wonderful added to soups, pastas, salads, or risottos, like I've done here. Don't sleep on it.

Preheat the oven to 375°F.

Put the tomatoes into an ovenproof dish with 2 tablespoons of the olive oil and some salt and roast for 20 to 25 minutes, or until just bursting.

Have your stock simmering on the stove and a large bowl of ice water nearby. Using tongs, dunk the wild garlic in the stock for 1 minute and then plunge it into the ice water. (You can skip this step if using basil.)

In a mortar and pestle, or using an immersion blender, combine the wild garlic (or basil), pine nuts, lemon juice, and nutritional yeast (or parmesan) with the olive oil until a pesto forms. Season to taste, adding more olive oil if needed to get the right consistency.

In a large pan, heat the remaining 1 tablespoon olive oil and sauté the shallot for 5 minutes. Follow with the garlic and sauté for 1 minute. Pour in the rice, stir to coat it in the oil, and then pour in the wine, add the butter, season with salt and pepper, and bring it to a simmer. Stir gently and when all the liquid has been absorbed by the rice, pour in a ladle of the hot stock. Stir gently, keeping the risotto simmering all the while. Repeat this process, stirring occasionally, until all the stock has been absorbed or until the rice is plump and al dente—this should take at least 25 minutes.

Meanwhile, prepare the bread crumbs: heat the olive oil in a frying pan and add the garlic and bread crumbs. Fry until golden—keep an eye on them so they don't burn!

When the rice is 90 percent cooked, stir in the pesto. Season to taste and finish with the roasted tomatoes, bread crumbs, and a squeeze of lemon.

TIP: To make this gluten free use GF bread crumbs.

SERVES 3 — GFO

14 oz / 400g cherry tomatoes on the vine

3 tbsp olive oil

1 quart / 1 liter hot vegetable stock

1 shallot, finely diced

1 garlic clove, crushed to a paste

1½ cups / 300g arborio rice

1 cup / 240ml dry white wine

1 knob of butter (or vegan alternative)

Lemon juice, to taste

Salt and black pepper

FOR THE WILD GARLIC PESTO

Large bunch (3½ oz / 100g) of wild garlic (or use regular basil)

2 tbsp toasted pine nuts

Juice of ½ lemon

1 tbsp nutritional yeast or 2 tbsp freshly grated parmesan

7 tbsp / 100ml olive oil (or more as needed)

FOR THE BREAD CRUMBS

1 tbsp olive oil

1 garlic clove, finely chopped or grated

2 cups / 100g panko bread crumbs

MEAL PREP

If you have a busy job and want to save some money, putting a bit of time aside on the weekend to prepare some meals for the week ahead can be a real lifesaver. My very first job out of school was working in Harrods in the apothecary department, trying (and failing somewhat miserably—sales are not my forte) to sell haircare and skincare products. I remember spending an absolute fortune on lunches most days, so much so that my salary was just dwindling before my eyes. It was a double whammy, as my health was going down the drain as well as my money because I was opting for quick meal deals that weren't particularly loaded with nutrients.
I began preparing delicious, nutrient-rich meals to take into work and found myself feeling satiated and better energized to take on the afternoons. I still wasn't able to save that much though, as I was literally working in a consumer's paradise, and with my employee discount I always found something to spend my earnings on. This chapter will help you to make your weeks run that little bit smoother and keep you feeling full and happy throughout the working day.

CHIPOTLE BLACK BEAN BOWL

I'm slightly obsessed with this bowl of food; it makes an appearance at least once a week in our household. It has all your major food groups and will keep you full and energized throughout the day.

Start by preheating the oven to 400°F.

Put the rice in a fine-mesh sieve and give it a good rinse, then put into a medium saucepan with a lid, pour in the water and add a pinch of salt. Bring it to a boil with the lid off, then lower the heat, clamp on the lid, and cook for 15 minutes before turning the heat off and letting it sit until the rest of the meal is ready.

Lay the cubed sweet potato on a baking sheet, drizzle with 1 tablespoon of the olive oil, season with salt and pepper, and roast in the oven for 35 to 40 minutes, until soft and caramelized. Drain the canned corn and put it on a separate baking sheet drizzled with the other 1 tablespoon of olive oil and some salt, then put it in the oven with the sweet potato and roast until charred—this should take about 15 minutes.

Put the diced onion, tomatoes, avocado, and black beans into a large bowl and stir gently to combine. Once cooked, add the sweet potato, corn, and rice to the bowl.

In a separate small bowl, mix together the dressing ingredients, loosening with a splash of water if needed. Pour the dressing over the salad and mix well. Serve scattered with the cilantro and chile (if using) and with lime wedges for squeezing over the top.

TIP: Using pre-cooked, packaged rice that you can reheat in the microwave will speed up the process.

MAKES 3 PORTIONS — GF

2 cups / 400g white rice (or your rice of choice)

2½ cups / 600ml water

1 large sweet potato, cut into ¾-inch / 2cm cubes

2 tbsp olive oil

½ x 15¼-oz / 432g can corn

½ red onion, diced

6⅓ oz / 180g tomatoes, diced

1 avocado, peeled, pitted, and diced

1 x 15-oz / 425g can black beans, drained and rinsed

Big handful of cilantro

1 red chile, sliced (optional)

Lime wedges

Salt and black pepper

FOR THE DRESSING

2 tbsp mayo

1 heaped tsp chipotle paste

Juice of 1 lime

SPICY KOREAN TOFU RICE BOWL

If you like spicy, then this one is for you. Gochujang is a wonderful Korean fermented chile paste and it packs a punch! Pairing it with the crunchy slaw and fresh pickled cucumbers really lifts the flavors.

Preheat the oven to 375°F.

Mix together the gochujang, rice wine vinegar, soy sauce, honey, and lime juice in a small bowl. Line a baking sheet with parchment paper and lay your tofu cubes on top. Pour half the marinade over the tofu, ensuring it is covered well. Roast in the oven for 10 minutes, then pour the remaining marinade over the tofu and return to the oven for 10 more minutes, until sticky and caramelized.

In separate bowls, mix together the slaw ingredients, and cover the cucumber with the vinegar, sugar, and salt. Let them pickle while the tofu cooks.

Put the rice in a fine-mesh sieve and give it a good rinse, then put into a medium saucepan with a lid. Pour in the water and add a pinch of salt. Bring it to a boil with the lid off, then lower the heat, clamp on the lid, and cook for 15 minutes before turning the heat off and letting it sit until the rest of the meal is ready.

Cook the Broccolini in a saucepan of boiling water for 3 to 4 minutes and then plunge into a bowl of ice water to keep its vibrant green color. Drain and pat dry. (You can skip plunging into ice water if you intend to eat it as soon as you've cooked it.)

Once everything is cooked, load up your bowls with each component and sprinkle with the sliced green onion and sesame seeds. Store in the fridge for up to 3 days.

TIP: To make this gluten free use GF soy sauce.

MAKES 3 TO 4 PORTIONS — GFO

1 heaped tbsp gochujang paste

1 tbsp rice wine vinegar

1 tbsp soy sauce

2 tsp honey (or sweetener of choice)

Juice of ½ lime

1 x 1 lb / 454g block of firm tofu, cut into ½-inch / 1cm cubes

1½ cups / 300g jasmine rice

2½ cups / 600ml water

9 oz / 250g Broccolini

1 green onion, sliced, to garnish

Sesame seeds, to garnish

FOR THE SLAW

½ red cabbage, shredded

1 tbsp vegan mayo (or egg-based alternative)

Juice of ½ lime

Pinch of salt

FOR THE PICKLED CUCUMBER

1 small cucumber, sliced into rounds

3 tbsp rice wine vinegar

1 tsp sugar

1 tsp salt

QUINOA, PONZU, AND EDAMAME SALAD

M&S, a beloved British retailer, used to do a salad like this and then for some very sad reason they discontinued it. I was beside myself, so I had to try re-create it. I think I've come pretty close because this salad is addictive!

Rinse the quinoa under cold water, put it into a saucepan with a lid, then top it up with water so it sits about a ½ inch / 1cm above the quinoa line. Add the stock cube and bring to a boil, then decrease the heat to low, put the lid on, and let it simmer for 20 minutes, or until tender and fluffy and all the liquid has been absorbed.

Cook the edamame in a medium saucepan of boiling water for 5 minutes and then drain and plunge into cold water to retain their green color. Drain and pat dry.

Put all the diced, shredded, and sliced vegetables into a bowl along with the cooked quinoa and edamame. Drain the chickpeas and add these too.

In a separate bowl, mix together all the dressing ingredients and pour over the salad.

Top with sesame seeds and store in the fridge for up to 3 days.

TIP: To make this gluten free use GF ponzu or soy sauce.

MAKES 3 PORTIONS
— GFO

¾ cup plus 2 tbsp / 150g quinoa

½ vegetable stock cube

1⅓ cups / 200g shelled edamame

½ large cucumber, diced

1 large carrot, shredded

2 red bell peppers, seeded and diced

5 green onions, sliced

1 avocado, peeled, pitted, and diced

1 x 15-oz / 425g can chickpeas

Sesame seeds, to garnish

FOR THE DRESSING

3 tbsp sesame oil

3 tbsp ponzu
(or 2 tbsp soy sauce and 1 tbsp lemon juice)

1 tbsp rice wine vinegar

1 tsp honey (or sweetener of choice)

Juice of ½ lemon

1 tsp grated ginger

ROMESCO ROASTED VEG QUINOA BOWL

This dish works really well hot or cold. I tend to make it for dinner and then box up the rest for the following days. You can use whatever veg you have available, but my favorites are broccoli and zucchini!

Preheat the oven to 375°F.

Mix all the fresh veg with the olive oil, herbs, and paprika and season with salt. Place on a baking sheet and roast in the oven for 25 minutes.

Meanwhile, rinse the quinoa and place in a pan with the crumbled stock cube. Cover with enough cold water so it sits ½ inch / 1cm above the quinoa. Bring it to a boil and then clamp the lid on, turn the heat down, and let it simmer for 20 minutes, or until tender and fluffy and all the liquid has been absorbed.

Meanwhile, blitz all the romesco sauce ingredients together until smooth in a high-speed blender.

Tip the quinoa into a bowl. Pat the chickpeas dry and stir them into the cooked quinoa.

Divide the romesco sauce evenly over the bottoms of 3 or 4 containers. Top with the quinoa and roasted veg and finish with the sliced almonds and chopped parsley.

TIP: If you have a nut allergy, swap the almonds for sunflower seeds.

MAKES 3 TO 4 PORTIONS — GF

1 small head of broccoli (9 oz / 250g), cut into florets

2 red onions, cut into ½ inch / 1cm thick slices

1 large zucchini (10½ oz / 300g), chopped the same size as the broccoli

1 tbsp olive oil

1 tbsp fresh oregano, chopped

1 tbsp fresh parsley, chopped

1 tsp smoked paprika

Scant 1 cup / 150g tricolored quinoa

1 vegetable stock cube, crumbled

1 x 15-oz / 425g can chickpeas, drained and rinsed

Salt and black pepper

FOR THE ROMESCO SAUCE

¾ cup / 100g blanched almonds

1 x 16 fl oz / 473ml jar roasted red bell peppers (about 12¾ oz / 360g drained weight)

1 garlic clove

1 tbsp nutritional yeast or freshly grated parmesan

1 tsp sherry vinegar (or red wine vinegar)

1 tsp olive oil

Pinch of salt

TO SERVE

¼ cup / 30g sliced almonds

Chopped parsley

MEDITERRANEAN "FETA" COUSCOUS SALAD

I used to have a bit of a love–hate relationship with couscous but my partner, Cameron, absolutely loves it, so I tried a few different things and eventually came up with this recipe, which I now love too. Roasting vegetables in plenty of olive oil until they're bursting and juicy and then stirring them into the couscous is the key.

Preheat the oven to 375°F.

If you're making the tofu "feta," put the tofu chunks into a lidded plastic container with the remaining "feta" ingredients. Put the lid on, give it a good shake, and set aside to marinate until you're ready to serve.

Put the diced zucchini, red bell peppers, and tomatoes in a roasting dish with the olive oil and some salt and roast for 25 minutes.

Meanwhile, put all the ingredients for the roasted chickpeas in a separate roasting dish, toss to coat, and roast in the oven alongside the veg until crisp, 20 to 25 minutes.

Place the couscous in a large bowl, sprinkle in the stock cube, oregano, and parsley, and top with enough boiling water to sit ½ inch / 1cm above the line of the couscous. Place a plate on top of the bowl and let it sit for 10 minutes, until all the water is absorbed. Remove the lid and fluff the couscous with a fork.

Put the sliced onion into a bowl and squeeze the lemon juice over the top and a touch of salt. Let rest for 5 minutes before squeezing with your fingers, to pickle it.

Once the vegetables in the oven have broken down and become juicy, mix them into the couscous along with the roasted chickpeas so that everything is evenly dispersed.

Serve in bowls or portion into lidded plastic containers, topped with the "feta," pickled onion, and another squeeze of lemon.

MAKES 3 PORTIONS — GFO

1 large zucchini, diced

3 red bell peppers, seeded and diced

5¼ oz / 150g cherry tomatoes, diced

1 tbsp olive oil

1 cup / 180g dried couscous

¼ vegetable stock cube

1 tsp dried oregano

1 tsp dried parsley (or use 1 tbsp chopped fresh parsley)

½ tsp red pepper flakes

½ red onion, sliced into half-moons

Juice of ½ lemon

Salt

FOR THE TOFU "FETA" (OR USE REAL FETA)

14 oz / 400g firm tofu, torn into rough chunks

1 tbsp nutritional yeast

1 tsp dried oregano

½ tsp onion granules

½ tsp garlic granules

Squeeze of lemon

Pinch of salt

1 tsp olive oil

FOR THE ROASTED CHICKPEAS

1 x 15-oz / 425g can chickpeas, drained and rinsed

1 tbsp olive oil

½ tsp smoked paprika

½ tsp ground cumin

1 tsp dried oregano

½ tsp garlic granules

Pinch of salt

TIP: Use a glass/transparent bowl when preparing the couscous to ensure you get the water/couscous ratio right. To make this gluten free swap the couscous for your choice of rice.

SPRING PASTA SALAD

Pasta salad is a classic and makes the perfect on-the-go lunch. This one is light, fresh, and summery and a favorite in our house.

Bring a large saucepan of water to a boil and have a bowl of ice water ready. Drop the asparagus and peas into the boiling water and cook for about 2 minutes. Scoop them out with a slotted spoon and transfer to the bowl of ice water. Once they are completely cool, drain and pat dry.

Add the stock cube to the pan of boiling water and cook your pasta in it until al dente, usually 9 to 12 minutes (depending on the shape you use).

Meanwhile, heat 1 tablespoon of the olive oil in a large frying pan over medium heat and sauté the lardons until crisp and delicious.

Drain the pasta, reserving a mug of the cooking water, and add the pasta to the pan of lardons. Pour in a little bit of the water to emulsify the sauce and then let cool completely for about half an hour before stirring in the asparagus and peas.

Drizzle with the remaining 1 tablespoon olive oil and squeeze the lemon juice over the top. Tear and scatter the basil leaves, season to taste, and then portion up into containers.

TIP: Use GF pasta to make this gluten free.

MAKES 3 PORTIONS
— GFO

7 oz / 200g asparagus, sliced into 1-inch / 2.5cm lengths

⅔ cup / 100g frozen peas

1 vegetable stock cube

12¼ oz / 350g farfalle pasta (or use penne, rigatoni, fusilli)

2 tbsp olive oil

5¼ oz / 150g bacon lardons (real or plant-based)

Juice of 1 lemon

Handful of fresh basil leaves

Salt and black pepper

MISO TOFU RICE BOWL

Black rice was once nicknamed "forbidden rice" because in ancient China it was considered so nutritious and unique that it was forbidden to eat it unless you were a member of the royal family. Its dark purple hue means it is rich in disease-fighting antioxidants and when paired with the rest of the ingredients in this bowl it will promote healthy digestion and heart health and have you glowing from the inside out.

Preheat the oven to 400°F and line a baking sheet with parchment paper.

Mix together the dressing ingredients in a bowl, loosening with water to a dropping consistency.

Pat the tofu dry with paper towels, then cut into ½-inch / 1cm cubes. Put it into a bowl with the cornstarch and 2 tablespoons of the dressing and mix gently to coat. Arrange the tofu pieces on the lined baking sheet and bake for 30 minutes until browning around the edges.

Rinse the rice, put it into a saucepan, and cover with three times the volume of water. Bring it to a boil and then lower to a simmer, clamp the lid on, and cook for 20 minutes, or until the rice is tender. Drain and let it stand for a moment to steam.

While the rice is cooking, put the red cabbage into a bowl with 2 tablespoons of the dressing to make a slaw. Put a kettle of water on to boil.

Once the rice is done, portion it out into bowls or containers. Put the Broccolini and edamame into the empty rice pan, cover with boiling water from the kettle, and cook for 4 minutes, then plunge into ice water to retain the bright green color. (If eating immediately, skip the plunge!)

Add the tofu, Broccolini, edamame, and cabbage to your bowls or containers, drizzle with the remaining dressing, and top with the sliced green onion and sesame seeds.

MAKES 3 PORTIONS
— GF

1 x 14-oz / 400g block of firm tofu

1 tbsp cornstarch

2½ cups / 500g black rice

½ red cabbage, finely shredded

10½ oz / 300g Broccolini

2 cups / 300g frozen shelled edamame

1 green onion, sliced, to garnish

Sesame seeds, to garnish

FOR THE DRESSING

¼ cup / 65g white miso paste

¼ cup / 60ml sesame oil

2 tbsp rice wine vinegar

Juice of ½ lemon

1 tbsp honey (or sweetener of choice)

Water, as needed

QUINOA, SQUASH, AND BROCCOLINI SALAD

Tahini and squash work so well together and with the addition of bursting jewels of pomegranate seeds this dish really sings, brightening up your packed lunch beyond recognition.

Preheat the oven to 375°F.

Tip the squash onto a baking sheet, drizzle with the olive oil, season with salt and pepper, and roast in the oven for 25 to 30 minutes, until tender.

Meanwhile, rinse the quinoa under cold water to remove any excess starch. Place in a saucepan with the stock cube and fill with water to ½ inch / 1cm above the quinoa line. Bring to a boil and then put the lid on, turn down the heat, and simmer for 20 minutes.

Bring another saucepan of water to a boil and have ready a bowl of ice water. Trim the woody ends off the Broccolini and boil for 4 minutes, then drain and dunk in the ice water before patting dry and cutting into bite-size pieces.

In a separate bowl, mix together the tahini, lemon juice, and honey until a thick paste forms. Loosen it with cold water to reach your desired dressing consistency.

Once the quinoa, Broccolini, and squash are all cooked, mix them together in a large bowl, then top with the tahini dressing, pomegranate seeds, and pumpkin seeds. Portion out into three containers and store in the fridge for up to 3 days.

MAKES 3 PORTIONS — GF

1 butternut squash, peeled, seeded, and cut into crescents

1 to 2 tbsp olive oil

Scant 1 cup / 150g tricolored quinoa

1 vegetable stock cube

7 oz / 200g Broccolini

3 tbsp tahini

Juice of ½ lemon

1 tsp honey (or sweetener of choice)

Cold water, as needed

2 tbsp pomegranate seeds

2 tbsp pumpkin seeds

Salt and black pepper

PESTO, LEMON, AND PEA ORZO

Orzo is such a great-shaped pasta, its rice-iness making it perfect for salads or even to use in a risotto. This fresh, lemony number is a great lunch or dinner and stores well. Just be sure to leave the arugula on top so it doesn't get soggy!

Bring a large saucepan of water to a boil and have a large bowl of ice water ready. Boil the peas for 3 minutes and then scoop them out with a slotted spoon and transfer to the ice water. Once they are completely cool, drain and pat dry.

Add the stock cube to the large pan of boiling water and pour in the orzo. Cook for 8 to 10 minutes, or until al dente.

Meanwhile, either in a food processor or mortar and pestle, combine all the pesto ingredients by whizzing them up or bashing them. Season to taste.

Once the orzo is cooked, drain and tip into a mixing bowl before stirring in the pesto and peas.

Portion the orzo out into containers and top with the arugula and toasted pine nuts.

TIP: You can swap the orzo with any GF pasta to make it gluten free.

MAKES 3 PORTIONS
— GFO

1⅓ cups / 200g frozen peas

1 vegetable stock cube

1⅓ cups / 250g orzo

2 big handfuls of arugula

2 tbsp toasted pine nuts

FOR THE PESTO

4 big handfuls of fresh basil

1 tbsp nutritional yeast

Juice of ½ lemon

3 tbsp olive oil

Salt and black pepper

MISO SOBA NOODLE SALAD

This was one of my most popular meals during my time working in the Bahamas. It works perfectly as one to make ahead because it is best served cold, so you can grab it from the fridge just before you want to eat. It's refreshing and nutritious and you can use whatever veg you have on hand.

Bring a large saucepan of water to a boil, add the soba noodles, and let them cook for 5 to 7 minutes. While they are cooking, get a bowl of ice water ready to plunge them into. Once they are done, remove using tongs and plunge into the ice water to stop the cooking process; this will also wash away the starchiness and prevent them from sticking together. Squeeze out all the water from the noodles and set aside in a large bowl ready to mix with the rest of the salad.

Tip the edamame into the same pan of boiling water and cook until tender, then drain and plunge them into the ice water to retain their green color. Drain and tip into the bowl with the noodles along with the radishes, carrots, and red cabbage.

In a separate bowl, mix together the dressing ingredients, loosening with a little water if needed.

Pour the dressing over the noodles and veg and mix well. Portion it out into your containers and top with the sliced green onion, sesame seeds, and a wedge of lime.

TIP: Make sure you use rice noodles if you want to make this gluten free.

MAKES 3 PORTIONS — GFO

9 oz / 250g dried soba noodles (or any preferred noodle)

2 cups / 300g shelled edamame

7 oz / 200g radishes, sliced

2 large carrots, shredded

½ red cabbage, thinly sliced

FOR THE DRESSING

¼ cup / 65g white miso paste

¼ cup / 60ml sesame oil

2 tbsp rice wine vinegar

Juice of ½ lemon

1 tbsp honey (or sweetener of choice)

Water, as needed

TO FINISH

1 green onion, sliced

Sesame seeds

Lime wedges

143

HONEY MUSTARD PUY LENTIL SALAD

This for me is an oldie but a goldie. This was one of the first salads I ever made as meal prep when I was working at Harrods. It saw me through a lot of long shifts and kept me nourished and satiated; it's still one I turn to when I know I'm going to have a busy week ahead. This salad also works brilliantly with the addition of some flaked cooked salmon or shredded roasted chicken.

Put the lentils into a saucepan and cover with 3 cups of water. Bring to a boil, then lower the heat and simmer for 20 minutes, until just tender. Drain and set aside.

Cut the avocado into cubes, tip into a bowl, and squeeze the lemon juice over the top.

Bring another saucepan of water to a boil and have ready a bowl of ice water. Cook the Broccolini and green beans in the boiling water for 3 to 4 minutes before plunging them into the ice water to halt the cooking process and preserve their green color. Drain and pat dry.

In a separate bowl, mix together the dressing ingredients and then spoon evenly into the bottom of three lidded containers so that when stored, nothing goes soggy. Layer the lentils on top, followed by the blanched greens, cherry tomatoes, avocado, a handful of arugula, the pumpkin seeds, and a sprinkle of salt. Store in the fridge for up to 3 days.

Just before eating, shake everything in the container to mix the dressing with the salad.

MAKES 3 PORTIONS — GF

Scant 1 cup / 180g Puy lentils

1 avocado

Juice of ½ lemon

5¼ oz / 150g Broccolini, trimmed and cut into bite-size pieces

3½ oz / 100g green beans, trimmed

2 handfuls of cherry tomatoes, halved

3 handfuls of arugula

3 tbsp pumpkin seeds

FOR THE DRESSING

¼ cup / 60ml olive oil

1 tbsp whole-grain mustard

1 tbsp honey

Juice of 1 lemon

1 tbsp white wine vinegar

Salt and black pepper

BREAKFAST, FAST

I feel this chapter doesn't need too much of an
introduction, other than to say here are some quick,
filling, and nutritious breakfasts for you when you
need to get out of the house as quickly as possible.
Breakfast is actually my favorite meal of the day,
so it's important to me to have options other than
cereal or a quick piece of toast. This echoes my ethos
on food being for pleasure and not just practicality.
Every mealtime should be enjoyed, regardless of
whether you're rushing out the door or not!

TROPICAL SMOOTHIE BOWL WITH GRANOLA

This refreshing, mood-boosting start to the day always makes me feel brand new after drinking it. The combination of the pineapple and mango feels so fresh and reviving—it's the perfect wake-up call.

Put all the smoothie ingredients into a high-powered blender and blitz until smooth. You may need to add a little bit of hot water from the kettle to help along the frozen bits.

Pour into a bowl and sprinkle with your toppings.

TIP: To make this gluten free make sure you use a GF granola.

SERVES 1 — GFO

Handful of frozen mango chunks

Handful of frozen pineapple chunks

Handful of frozen spinach

½ banana (fresh or frozen)

1⅔ cups / 400ml coconut water

1-inch / 2.5cm piece of ginger

TO TOP

Handful of granola (store-bought or page 166)

1 tsp chia seeds

1 tsp flaxseed

1 tsp toasted coconut flakes

SUPERFOOD SMOOTHIE

A smoothie is the ultimate on-the-go breakfast and can be loaded with so much good stuff. It's also a fun way to get kids interested in using different ingredients and making their own breakfasts. You can customize it to your liking but the ingredients selected here are loaded with antioxidants, omegas 3 and 6, and healthy fats to keep you feeling full and satisfied for the morning.

Blend everything up in a blender, adding more milk if necessary to reach your desired consistency. Enjoy!

TIP: Although oats don't naturally contain gluten, make sure to use GF oats if you are celiac.

SERVES 1 — GFO

1 banana

Handful of blueberries

Handful of raspberries

2 Brazil nuts

1 tsp ground flaxseed

1 tsp chia seeds

1 tsp hemp seeds
(or any other seeds)

2 tbsp rolled oats

1 tbsp honey (or to taste)

1⅔ cups / 400ml milk of choice

A TRIO OF QUICK TOASTS

TAHINI TOAST WITH HONEY AND BANANA

Tahini is one of those ingredients that lends itself so well to both savory and sweet recipes. The idea for this came from a lack of peanut butter in the house and tahini being the next best thing. It has been a staple ever since!

Toast the bread and then spread or pour the tahini and honey over the top. Top with the sliced banana and finish with the cinnamon and a pinch of salt.

TIP: With tahini, it's worth getting the best quality you can, which is usually indicated by texture—the runnier the better! To make this gluten free use GF bread.

SERVES 1 — GFO

1 slice of your choice of bread

2 tbsp tahini

2 tsp honey

1 large banana, sliced into rounds

½ tsp ground cinnamon

Pinch of salt

GUT-LOVING TOAST

Sauerkraut is something I can regularly be found eating straight out of the jar—it's the perfect gut-loving, salty snack! Having some in the morning will kick-start your digestion and set you up for a great day.

Pop your bread in the toaster while you prep the topping.

Mash the avocado with the olive oil and some salt and pepper and spread it on your toast. Top with the sauerkraut and seeds and enjoy.

TIP: To make this gluten free use GF bread.

SERVES 1 — GFO

1 slice of your choice of bread

½ avocado

1 tsp olive oil

2 tbsp sauerkraut

1 tsp pumpkin seeds

1 tsp hemp seeds (or any other seeds)

Salt and black pepper

TOFU SCRAMBLE WITH AVOCADO TOAST

I am a savory girl at heart so this is the breakfast I turn to the most. It hits all your macros (protein, carbs, and fats) and keeps you perfectly full until lunchtime.

Heat the olive oil in a frying pan and then crumble in the tofu and add the turmeric and garlic granules. Stir it around so it is all well mixed, then let it cook for about 5 minutes to allow it to get some crispy bits. Stir in the milk to make it a bit creamier. Season to taste, then set aside.

Pop the bread in the toaster while you smash up the avocado in a bowl along with a good squeeze of lemon juice and some salt and pepper. Spread this over the toast and top with the scramble, along with another squeeze of lemon juice, then sprinkle with the sesame seeds and chives and finish with a drizzle of hot sauce (if using).

TIP: To make this gluten free use GF bread.

SERVES 1 — GFO

1 tsp olive oil

3½ oz / 100g firm tofu

¼ tsp ground turmeric

½ tsp garlic granules

1 tbsp milk of choice

1 large slice of your choice of bread

½ avocado

Juice of ½ lemon

1 tsp sesame seeds

1 tbsp chopped chives

1 tsp hot sauce (optional)

Salt and black pepper

CHAI-SPICED APPLE PORRIDGE

The key to this is using quick-cook rolled oats; this will shave quite a few minutes off the cook time and give you a hearty, delicious breakfast in an instant.

Put the apple into a saucepan with the sugar and half the cinnamon. Cook over medium heat for 5 minutes, until the apple starts to get soft around the edges. Tip into a bowl and cover with foil to keep warm.

Pour the oats, milk, and remaining spices into the same saucepan and bring to a gentle simmer, stirring continuously until thick—this may take 5 to 10 minutes. Add a splash of water if you want it looser.

Serve the porridge in a bowl, topped with the apple, maple syrup, almond butter, and seeds.

TIP: Although oats don't naturally contain gluten, make sure to use GF oats if you are celiac.

SERVES 1 — GFO

1 apple, cored and diced

½ tsp light brown sugar

1 tsp ground cinnamon

½ cup / 50g quick-cooking rolled oats

7 tbsp / 100ml milk of choice

¼ tsp grated nutmeg

½ tsp ground ginger

¼ tsp ground cardamom

1 tsp maple syrup

1 tbsp almond butter

1 tsp chia seeds (or any other seeds you have on hand)

OVERNIGHT OATS, THREE WAYS

TIP: All three of these overnight oat recipes will keep well in the fridge for up to 4 days. Although oats don't naturally contain gluten, make sure to use GF oats if you are celiac.

MAPLE TAHINI OVERNIGHT OATS

The savoriness of the tahini paired with the maple syrup makes this so rich and delicious and it's one of my favorite on-the-go breakfasts! You can prep it the night before and store it in the fridge, ready to grab and go the following morning.

The night before, mix together the tahini, milk, and maple syrup until smooth. Add the oats, chia seeds, and flaxseed and mix well, adding a splash of water or more milk if you like a looser consistency. It will look more like a soup with oats in it but it will thicken overnight and become a homogenous, delicious consistency.

Pour into three containers and store in the fridge until ready to eat.

This is perfectly tasty on its own or topped with fruit like banana or berries.

MAKES 3 PORTIONS — GFO

¼ cup / 75g tahini

1¼ cups / 300ml milk of choice

2 tbsp maple syrup (or to taste)

1⅔ cups / 150g rolled oats

1 tbsp chia seeds

1 tbsp ground flaxseed

Sliced banana or mixed berries, to serve (optional)

CARROT CAKE OVERNIGHT OATS

This is like dessert for breakfast! The spices running throughout will wrap you up and give you a warm hug.

The night before, grate the carrot into a large bowl and then add the remaining ingredients. Mix well and add a splash of water or more milk if you prefer a looser consistency. It will look more like a soup with oats in it but it will thicken overnight and become a homogenous, delicious consistency.

Pour into three containers and store in the fridge until you are ready to eat.

MAKES 3 PORTIONS
— GFO

1 large carrot

1⅔ cups / 150g rolled oats

1⅔ cups / 400ml milk of choice

2 tbsp raisins

Handful of chopped walnuts

2 tbsp maple syrup

1 tsp cinnamon

½ tsp nutmeg

1 tbsp chia seeds

1 tbsp ground flaxseed

CHUNKY MONKEY OVERNIGHT OATS

Although I love each of these overnight oat recipes equally, I think it's hard to beat the combination of banana, peanut butter, and chocolate . . .

The night before, mix everything except the peanut butter and banana together in a large bowl. Add a splash of water or more milk if you prefer a looser consistency. It will look more like a soup with oats in it but it will thicken overnight and become a homogenous, delicious consistency.

Pour into three containers, swirl peanut butter on top of each one, and finish with the sliced banana. Store in the fridge until you wish to eat.

MAKES 3 PORTIONS
— GFO

1⅔ cups / 150g rolled oats

1⅔ cups / 400ml milk of choice

2 tbsp cacao nibs or chocolate chips

1 tbsp chia seeds

1 tbsp ground flaxseed

1 tbsp maple syrup

2 tbsp peanut butter

1 banana, sliced

159

LEMON AND BLUEBERRY CHIA POT

Chia pots, or chia puddings as they often get called, tend to be a bit like Marmite with the general public. You either love them or hate them and I'm usually in the latter camp, but this recipe is the exception. I like to use enough lemon to make you want to suck your cheeks in, but that is, of course, down to your personal preference. The lemon and blueberry combo keeps this fresh, light, and rather delicious—even if I do say so myself!

Mix the chia seeds with half the yogurt, the milk, lemon juice, and maple syrup and let stand for 5 minutes.

Prepare the three pots you want to serve in by filling the bottom of each evenly with blueberries and then top with the rest of the yogurt.

Once the thickened chia mixture is ready, spoon it evenly over your pots of yogurt. When you're ready to serve, sprinkle with granola (if using) and lemon zest.

TIP: You can store these in the fridge, covered, for up to 3 days. Although oats don't naturally contain gluten, make sure to use GF granola if you are celiac.

SERVES 3 — GFO

⅓ cup / 50g chia seeds

1¼ cups / 300g plain yogurt of choice

1½ cups / 360ml milk of choice (I use almond milk)

Juice and zest of ½ lemon

¼ cup / 60ml maple syrup

1 cup / 150g blueberries (ideally fresh, but frozen will work too)

Granola (store-bought or page 166), to top (optional)

BREAKFAST, SLOW

Slow breakfasts are special things to be savored and usually only feature on the weekends or on vacation for me, but there's no reason why they can't be enjoyed more often! Cameron and I have a Sunday ritual of a morning dog walk followed by a late brunch of a big stack of pancakes alongside a good cuppa and the crossword. This chapter is filled with many more of our favorite recipes to make on those lazy days.

HOMEMADE MAPLE GRANOLA

If you made this in advance, it could also be a part of the fast breakfast section—topped with yogurt, it's a great on-the-go breakfast. That said, we do love to have it slightly warm out of the oven!

Preheat the oven to 325°F and line a baking sheet with parchment paper.

Mix together the coconut oil and maple syrup.

In a large bowl, combine the oats, nuts, and seeds, and then pour the oil and maple syrup mixture over the top and combine well.

Pour out onto the prepared baking sheet and pat down; this will help create little clusters. Bake for 15 to 20 minutes—do not stir or mix around during baking! Let cool completely so that you retain the clusters.

Once cool, lift the parchment paper from both ends and slide the granola into your chosen container. Store in an airtight container at room temperature for up to 1 month.

TIP: Although oats don't naturally contain gluten, make sure to use GF oats if you are celiac.

MAKES ROUGHLY
15 PORTIONS — GFO

3 tbsp melted coconut oil

2 tbsp maple syrup

5½ cups / 500g rolled oats

¾ cup / 100g mixed nuts

⅔ cup / 80g mixed seeds

FLUFFY BUCKWHEAT PANCAKES AND DATE CARAMEL

I would say this is one of Cameron's favorite breakfasts. The date caramel is addictive and can be used on lots of things other than just the pancakes. I like it on toast, swirled into yogurt, or even on ice cream!

Put the dates in a bowl and cover with boiling water. Set aside while you prepare the pancake batter.

Mash the banana in a bowl until it is as smooth and wet as possible. Pour in the milk and maple syrup and whisk until combined. Sift in the buckwheat flour and baking powder and mix well until no lumps remain and it has a thick dropping consistency.

Put a frying pan over high heat and add a little butter, swirling it around to coat the bottom of the pan. Pour a ladle or two of the pancake mix onto the pan to create a pancake about 4 inches / 10cm in diameter. Once little bubbles appear on the top, it is time to flip. They will need about 1 minute on each side. Repeat with the remaining batter until it's all used up—you'll need to use a dot of butter each time you fry a new batch of pancakes.

Remove the dates from the water (do not throw the water away). Put the dates into a mini food processor (or use an immersion blender) and blitz, slowly adding the soaking liquid until a smooth caramel forms—up to 7 tablespoons / 100ml of water creates the right consistency. Season with a pinch of salt.

Serve the pancakes with the date caramel, yogurt, and blueberries, or your choice of fresh fruit.

SERVES 4 (MAKES 12 TO 15 PANCAKES)
— GF

FOR THE DATE CARAMEL

5 dates, pitted

Pinch of salt

FOR THE PANCAKES

1 ripe banana

1 cup / 240ml unsweetened milk of choice

1 tbsp maple syrup

1¼ cups / 140g buckwheat flour (blitz a heaped ¾ cup / 140g raw buckwheat groats in a blender, or use any flour you have on hand)

1 tsp baking powder

1½ tbsp butter (or vegan alternative)

TO SERVE

2 to 3 tbsp Greek or plain yogurt of choice

1½ cups / 250g blueberries, figs, or other fruit

171

A TRIO OF MY FAVORITE TOAST TOPPINGS

SMOKY BEANS ON TOAST

I would be lying if I said Heinz baked beans don't make a regular appearance in my household, but when we are feeling extra fancy, or we have guests over, Heinz is out and homemade is in.

Heat the olive oil in a large frying pan over medium heat, add the shallot and a pinch of salt, and sauté for 5 minutes, until softening. Add the garlic, smoked paprika, and cayenne pepper and fry for 1 minute or so.

Pour in the canned tomatoes and beans and add the sugar and Worcestershire sauce. Bring to a boil and then turn down to a simmer for 15 minutes, or until thick. Season to taste.

Serve the beans on top of the toast with a sprinkling of the fresh herbs.

TIP: To make this gluten free use GF Worcestershire sauce and bread.

SERVES 2 TO 3 — GFO

1 tbsp olive oil

½ shallot, diced

3 garlic cloves, finely chopped or grated

1 tsp smoked paprika

½ tsp cayenne pepper (or to taste)

1 x 14-oz / 400g can chopped tomatoes

1 x 15-oz / 425g can lima beans, drained and rinsed

Pinch of sugar

1 tsp Worcestershire sauce

2 to 3 slices of toasted sourdough or your choice of bread

1 tbsp chopped fresh chives or parsley

Salt and black pepper

BALSAMIC MUSHROOMS ON SOURDOUGH

Mushrooms on toast is a classic; I love it for breakfast and sometimes even for a quick lunch when I'm in a rush or craving something simple. It's one of those dishes you see in most places that serve breakfast but can be different every time you have it. This is my favorite way to make it, with a sweet balsamic twist!

In a dry frying pan, sauté the mushrooms with a pinch of salt until all the water has evaporated and the mushrooms begin to take on some color.

Add the olive oil and diced shallot and fry for 5 minutes more before adding the garlic. Cook this down for a couple of minutes and then add the balsamic vinegar. Let it bubble for a moment and then pour in the cream.

Season to taste and mix well, then pour on top of your toasted sourdough and finish with the chopped chives.

TIP: A fried or poached egg on top goes a long way! To make this gluten free use GF bread.

SERVES 2 — GFO

5¼ oz / 150g mushrooms, sliced (I use brown button or portobello)

Splash of olive oil

½ shallot, diced

3 garlic cloves, finely chopped or grated

1 tbsp balsamic vinegar

2 tbsp heavy cream of choice

2 slices of toasted sourdough or your choice of bread

2 tbsp chopped chives

Salt and black pepper

HARISSA BEANS ON TOAST WITH CHIVES AND SOUR CREAM

Beans on toast for breakfast is never a bad idea. These have a Middle Eastern slant and are wonderfully rich and flavorful. The perfect way to turn boring beans into a fancy breakfast.

Heat the olive oil in a large pan, add the shallot, and fry for 5 minutes over medium heat. Add the tomatoes, harissa paste, and garlic and cook for a few minutes, until the tomatoes are just starting to break down. Pour in the beans and the liquid from the can, season with salt and pepper, and bring to a boil. Immediately lower the heat and simmer for 5 minutes to thicken slightly.

Meanwhile, make the sour cream by mixing the yogurt, lemon juice, and a pinch of salt together in a bowl.

Toast the sourdough and top with the beans, a dollop of the sour cream, and a sprinkling of the fresh chives.

TIP: To make this gluten free use GF bread.

SERVES 2 — GFO

1 tbsp olive oil

1 shallot, diced

1¾ oz / 50g cherry or small tomatoes, halved

1 heaped tsp harissa paste

3 garlic cloves, finely chopped or grated

1 x 15-oz / 425g can lima beans

2 slices of sourdough or your choice of bread

2 tbsp chopped chives

Salt and black pepper

FOR THE SOUR CREAM

3 tbsp Greek yogurt of choice

Juice of ½ lemon

175

CACAO, BANANA, AND AVOCADO BOWL

This is inspired by a trip to Lisbon for Cameron's birthday a couple of years ago. We stumbled across a cute café that did the most incredible granola/smoothie bowls, one of them being this intensely smooth, chocolatey bowl that we immediately had to re-create when we got home. It's extremely rich and more like a pudding than a breakfast but it makes for a fabulous brunch!

Put all the ingredients (besides the toppings) into a high-speed blender with a splash of hot water and blitz until smooth and creamy. Add more hot water to break down the frozen ingredients if necessary.

Serve in bowls with your selection of toppings.

TIP: Although oats don't naturally contain gluten, make sure to use GF granola if you are celiac.

SERVES 2 — GFO

1 banana

1 frozen avocado

3 tbsp unsweetened cocoa powder

2 tbsp maple syrup

⅔ cup / 160ml milk of choice

Hot water, as needed

TO SERVE

Handful of granola (store-bought or page 166)

Berries

Mixed seeds

Nut butter

179

SAVORY BLACK BEAN BREAKFAST BOWL

I spent some time in Toronto, Canada with a client a few years ago and on my weekends off I would always go to this little chain called Kupfert & Kim. They served a Mexican-style breakfast bowl and I was completely obsessed. This is my version of it.

Preheat the oven to 400°F. Place the sweet potato on a baking sheet, drizzle with the olive oil and a sprinkle of salt, and roast for 35 to 40 minutes.

To make the beans, heat the olive oil in a frying pan and fry the shallot for 5 minutes over medium heat until softened. Add the garlic and spices and cook for 1 minute, stirring constantly. Pour in the beans and the liquid from the can, and add the oregano. Season to taste and bring to a gentle boil before turning down to a simmer for 5 to 10 minutes.

Put all the cashew cream ingredients into a high-speed blender and blitz until smooth, adding more water to loosen if necessary.

In a bowl, pickle the onion by squeezing in the lemon juice and sprinkling with salt. Let rest for 5 minutes and then squeeze with your fingers until the onion is bright pink.

For the scrambled tofu, heat the olive oil in a frying pan over medium heat, crumble in the tofu, and add the spices. Sauté for 3 to 4 minutes before adding the milk and stirring for 2 to 3 minutes more.

Assemble the bowl with all the elements, including the diced red bell pepper and avocado, and top with mixed seeds and hot sauce.

SERVES 2 — GF

1 small sweet potato, diced

1 tbsp olive oil

1 red bell pepper, seeded and diced

½ avocado, diced

Mixed seeds (sesame, sunflower, poppy), to serve

Hot sauce, to serve

FOR THE BEANS

1 tbsp olive oil

½ shallot, diced

4 garlic cloves, finely chopped or grated

1 tsp smoked paprika

½ tsp ground cumin

1 x 15-oz / 425g can black beans

1 tsp oregano

Salt and black pepper

FOR THE CASHEW CREAM

Handful of cashews

2 tbsp nutritional yeast

½ garlic clove

½ tsp white wine vinegar (or to taste)

¼ cup / 60ml water (plus more as needed)

Big pinch of salt

FOR THE PICKLED RED ONION

½ red onion, sliced into half-moons

Juice of ½ lemon

FOR THE SCRAMBLED TOFU

1 tbsp olive oil

6 oz / 175g firm tofu

¼ tsp ground turmeric

¼ tsp garlic granules

¼ tsp onion granules

½ tsp black salt (for egginess—optional)

¼ cup / 60ml milk of choice

BREAKFAST BRIOCHE BUN

This is my hangover special. Depending on the severity of the hangover, it often ends up being made past the traditional brunch hours, but once made, it's devoured within minutes and every second spent in the kitchen becomes worth it.

Preheat the oven to 375°F.

Start with the mushrooms: toss all the ingredients together in a bowl, season with salt and pepper, and air fry or roast in the oven until crisp, about 7 minutes in the air fryer, 25 to 30 minutes in the oven.

Pickle the red onion by covering with lemon juice and salt. Set aside for 5 minutes and then gently squeeze with your fingers until the onion turns light pink.

Put a frying pan over high heat, add the olive oil, and crumble in the tofu along with the turmeric, garlic and onion granules, and black salt (if using) and sauté for 3 minutes. Add the milk and sauté until it reaches a soft scrambled texture.

Season the avocado slices with salt and pepper.

Fill the toasted brioche buns with the avocado, tofu scramble, mushrooms, and pickled red onion, then cover with plenty of hot sauce!

TIP: Use GF buns and soy sauce to make this gluten free.

SERVES 2 — GFO

1 tbsp olive oil

5 oz / 140g firm tofu

Generous pinch of ground turmeric

¼ tsp garlic granules

¼ tsp onion granules

¼ tsp black salt (for egginess—optional)

¼ cup / 60ml milk of choice

½ avocado, sliced

2 brioche buns, toasted

Hot sauce

Salt and black pepper

FOR THE MUSHROOMS

2 portobello mushrooms, thickly sliced

1 tbsp liquid smoke (optional)

1 tbsp soy sauce

1 tsp balsamic vinegar

1 tsp olive oil

FOR THE PICKLED RED ONION

½ red onion, sliced into half-moons

Juice of ½ lemon

CHEESY CREPES

Quite often when we have crepes, we start with savory and then move on to sweet—almost like dinner to dessert. The fillings are totally customizable to what you have in your fridge; having cheese, however, is non-negotiable.

Fry the mushrooms in a dry frying pan with a pinch of salt until all their moisture has evaporated, then add 1 tablespoon of olive oil and cook until caramelized. Add the onion, spinach, and tomatoes and fry for 5 minutes more, tossing together until the spinach has wilted down. Season to taste, then remove from the pan.

Meanwhile, mix together the batter ingredients in a bowl until you have a thin dropping consistency. Heat a large spoonful of oil in a clean nonstick frying pan; once hot, pour in a ladle of the batter. Tilt the pan so the batter reaches the edges and cook for 3 to 4 minutes on one side, then flip over.

Add some of the filling to the cooked side, along with a healthy sprinkle of cheese, and let that cook for a couple of minutes before folding the crepe in half. Carefully flip again to cook the side that was on top for 1 minute before serving hot. Repeat with the remaining batter and filling.

TIP: Use GF flour to make this gluten free.

MAKES 3 TO 4 CREPES — GFO

¾ cup plus 3 tbsp / 115g all-purpose flour

1 cup plus 2 tbsp / 270ml milk of choice

Pinch of salt

Sunflower oil, for frying

FOR THE FILLING

9 oz / 250g mushrooms, roughly chopped

1 tbsp olive oil

½ red onion, diced

2 big handfuls of spinach, roughly chopped

Handful of cherry tomatoes, diced

1¾ oz / 50g cheddar or vegan alternative, grated

Salt and black pepper

BABUSHKA'S BLINIS WITH BERRY COMPOTE

I'm half Russian on my father's side and we used to visit my grandparents and extended family in Russia quite often. I was young and had an underdeveloped palate, which meant that my desire to sample the Russian cuisine was minuscule, so I lived mostly off my babushka's blinis (or grandma's pancakes, in English). She made them by the dozen and my brothers and I would slather them in compote, roll them up, and go exploring in the garden.

Start by preparing the compote. Put the berries and sugar into a saucepan, add the water, and place over medium heat. Stir the berries occasionally and let them break down until the mixture resembles a sauce. Remove from the heat and set aside to cool slightly while you make the blinis.

Mix together the flour, milk, maple syrup, and salt in a bowl until very smooth. Heat the oil in a nonstick frying pan over high heat and tilt to cover the surface of the pan before ladling in just enough batter to create a thin layer across the whole pan. Let it cook for 2 minutes or so before flipping and cooking for 1 minute on the other side. Repeat with the rest of the mixture until you have 6 or more pancakes piled on a plate.

Serve the blinis with the compote on top.

TIP: I would keep the plate in the oven on low heat so that the blinis stay warm until you've cooked them all. Use all-purpose GF flour to make these gluten free.

MAKES 6 TO 8 BLINIS
— GFO

1½ cups / 200g all-purpose flour

2 cups / 480ml milk of choice

3 tbsp maple syrup

Pinch of salt

1 tsp sunflower oil

FOR THE BERRY COMPOTE

1 cup / 150g mixed berries of choice

½ tbsp sugar

Splash of water

DIPS AND SIDES

A good dip is something you will always find in our fridge at home. They're the perfect snack for when you are so ravenous that if you don't have something to eat immediately someone is going to get hurt. I love them because they are so versatile: you can eat them with crunchy veg, chips, or bread, and they can usually be served alongside most meals. Dips make an appearance at almost every dinner party I host, so naturally I combined them in this chapter with all my favorite side dishes. If you're hosting a group of friends or even just an intimate dinner for two, this section of the book will hopefully help you create a wonderful spread of delights for your guests to enjoy.

HEIRLOOM TOMATOES AND SALSA VERDE

When the earliest of the tomatoes begin to ripen in summer, this is always the first recipe on the roster. I would urge you to get the best possible heirloom tomatoes available—I promise each morsel will bring you endless joy.

Begin by grating the garlic into a bowl and pouring in the lemon juice. Let sit for 5 minutes while you prepare the herbs.

Add the chopped capers and herbs to the same bowl as the garlic, cover with the olive oil, and season to taste, adding more lemon juice if you think it needs it.

Slice the tomatoes and lay them on a plate, then cover with the herb sauce and serve immediately.

TIP: Mop up any leftover salsa with bread—it's delicious!

SERVES 2 TO 3 AS
PART OF A SHARING
PLATE — GF

1 garlic clove

Juice of 1 lemon

Small bunch of chives, finely chopped

Small bunch of basil, finely chopped

Small bunch of parsley, finely chopped

1 tbsp capers, drained, rinsed, and finely chopped

5 to 6 tbsp olive oil

3 to 4 large heirloom tomatoes

Salt and black pepper

BROCCOLINI WITH TAHINI AND DUKKAH

I often make this for dinner parties as part of a mezze platter. My usual style is having all the food in the middle of the table for everyone to reach for and enjoy at their leisure and this dish is always a stand-out favorite. The combination of the tahini drizzle and the dukkah makes it look like a piece of art.

Preheat the oven to 400°F.

Place the Broccolini on a baking sheet with space between each stem. Drizzle with the olive oil, season with a little salt, and roast for 20 minutes.

Meanwhile, mix together the tahini, lemon juice, honey, and a good pinch of salt. Add a little water as needed to achieve a thick but pourable sauce.

Once the Broccolini is nice and crispy, transfer to a serving plate, drizzle with the tahini sauce, sprinkle with the dukkah, and serve immediately.

SERVES 2 AS A SIDE
— GF

5¼ oz / 150g Broccolini, trimmed

2 tbsp olive oil

2 tbsp tahini

Juice of ½ lemon

½ tsp honey (or to taste)

1 tbsp dukkah

Salt

Water, as needed

ROASTED RED-SKINNED POTATOES, CRISPY ONIONS, AND CHIVES

These potatoes are addictive! The salty, crispy onions on top are just so craveable you might devour the whole plate alone! Using the red-skinned potato gives a little more structure to your roasties but a Yukon Gold or russet would do the job just as well. Leave the skin on for extra nutrients.

Preheat the oven to 400°F.

Cut the potatoes into ½-inch / 1cm wedges, then transfer to a saucepan and cover with cold water and a good pinch of salt. Bring to a boil with the lid on. Once it reaches a rolling boil, drain the potatoes, return them to the pan, and let them steam dry, with the lid off, for 5 minutes.

Pour the olive oil into a large, deep baking dish and put into the oven to heat up for 5 minutes.

Put the lid back on the potatoes and give them a quick shake to break up the edges. Bring the baking dish out of the oven and carefully tip the roughed-up potatoes into the hot oil—the more space they have between them, the crispier they will get. Turn each wedge over in the oil and return the dish to the oven to roast for 35 minutes.

Remove the dish from the oven, scatter the sliced onions over the top, and return everything to the oven to roast for 20 to 25 minutes more, keeping an eye on the onions so they don't burn.

Serve fresh out of the oven, sprinkled with salt and the chives.

SERVES 4 AS A SIDE
— GF

1¾ lb / 800g red-skinned potatoes

5 to 6 tbsp olive oil

2 onions, thinly sliced

Small bunch of chives, finely chopped

Salt

WHIPPED FETA, ZUCCHINI, AND MINT

Summer, to me, means sunshine, entertaining, and small plates—lots of them. Whipped feta is the perfect base for most things but when zucchini are in season and are fried to perfection, they make a wonderful topping. Plus, it has my trifecta of ingredients: lemon, chile, and garlic, so it will always be a winner in my eyes.

Put the feta, Greek yogurt, and garlic into a bowl along with a small pinch of salt (the feta is salty). Blend with an immersion blender until smooth and then spread on a serving plate and sprinkle with some black pepper.

Heat the olive oil in a frying pan over high heat and fry the zucchini rounds for 1 to 2 minutes per side. Layer the fried zucchini on top of the whipped feta and drizzle with any remaining juice from the pan.

Squeeze the lemon juice over the top, then sprinkle with the lemon zest, chopped chile, and torn mint leaves. Finish with another drizzle of olive oil and some more black pepper.

SERVES 2 TO 3 AS
A SIDE — GF

7 oz / 200g feta cheese of choice

¼ cup / 70g Greek yogurt of choice

1 garlic clove, crushed to a paste

1 tbsp olive oil, plus extra for drizzling

2 medium zucchini (12¼ oz / 350g), sliced into ½-inch / 1cm rounds

Juice and zest of ½ lemon

1 red chile, finely chopped

Big handful of fresh mint leaves, torn

Salt and black pepper

199

MISO LEEKS AND BREAD CRUMBS

The sweetness of the leeks paired with the savory, umami notes of the miso works so beautifully in this dish. The bread crumbs give it a glorious crunch.

Start by preparing the bread crumbs. Heat the olive oil in a frying pan and sauté the garlic and chile for a couple of minutes before sprinkling in the bread crumbs along with a pinch of salt. Fry these until golden and season to taste—keep them moving so as not to burn them. Set aside on paper towels to soak up any excess oil while you get on with the rest.

Heat 1 tablespoon of the olive oil in a large frying pan. Place the leek rounds into the pan, cut side down, along with a pinch of salt. Fry over medium-high heat for 5 to 7 minutes, until they become charred. Turn them over, drizzle with the remaining 1 tablespoon olive oil and fry for another 5 minutes, until they become soft.

Once the leeks are cooked, mix the butter, miso, and honey together, then spoon this over the cooked leeks to melt. Swirl the pan so it reaches all the leeks.

Transfer the leeks to a plate, spoon over any leftover miso butter, then cover with the bread crumbs.

TIP: To make this gluten free either buy or make your own GF bread crumbs.

SERVES 2 AS A SIDE — GFO

2 tbsp olive oil

1 lb 2 oz / 500g leeks, rinsed and sliced into 1-inch / 2.5cm rounds

1½ tbsp butter (or vegan alternative), softened

1 tsp white miso paste

1 tsp honey

FOR THE BREAD CRUMBS

2 tbsp olive oil

1 garlic clove, finely chopped or grated

1 red chile, diced

½ cup / 50g dried bread crumbs

Salt

ZINGY CUCUMBER AND TAHINI SALAD

This combination of creamy tahini dressing with fresh cucumber and spice from the chile is a real whirlwind on the taste buds! It comes together so quickly and really packs a punch. This is the perfect summery salad: the cucumber feels fresh and hydrating while the tahini gives it a luxurious creaminess.

Cut the cucumber in half lengthwise and scoop out and discard the watery seeds in the middle. Lay the cucumber halves skin side up on a chopping board. Using a rolling pin or the handle of your knife (be careful), smack the cucumbers to form cracks — these will help absorb the flavor. Cut them into rough chunks and put into a bowl along with the sesame oil, rice wine, chile oil, honey, lime juice, and a good pinch of salt. Mix well to coat the cucumbers and let marinate while you make the tahini dressing.

In a separate bowl, whisk up the tahini, lemon juice, and salt, adding a splash of cold water to loosen if it is too thick. Whisk for about 5 minutes (if your arm can bear it), until a lighter color is achieved. You want quite a thick consistency so try not to add too much water and add it slowly.

Spread the thick tahini on a plate, top with the cucumbers and any leftover marinade, and finish with the green onions, crispy fried onions, chile, and sesame seeds.

TIP: To make this gluten free, make sure you use GF crispy fried onions.

SERVES 2 TO 3 AS A SIDE — GFO

1 large cucumber

1 tbsp toasted sesame oil

1 tsp Shaoxing rice wine (or white wine vinegar)

1 tsp crispy chile oil (or any chile oil)

1 tsp honey

Juice of 1 lime

3 green onions, thinly sliced

2 tbsp crispy fried onions

1 red chile, thinly sliced

1 tbsp black and white sesame seeds

Pinch of salt

FOR THE TAHINI DRESSING

Heaped ¼ cup / 70g tahini

Juice of 1 lemon

Pinch of salt

Cold water, as needed

CRISPY SMASHED NEW POTATOES ON ROMESCO SAUCE

Crispy roasted potatoes are never a bad idea. Even better when they sit on a punchy sauce with a tangy, herby dressing on top! These make a wonderful addition to a summer barbecue spread. Using peppers that come from a jar makes it so easy and less time-consuming to prepare, but you can always roast the peppers on a fire yourself.

Preheat the oven to 400°F.

Cut the potatoes so they are all roughly the same size—about 1½ inches / 4cm. Put them into a large saucepan, cover with cold water and a big pinch of salt, and bring to a boil. Parboil them until they are just soft enough to pierce with a fork, about 3 minutes after the water has reached a rolling boil. Drain carefully and let them steam in the pan with the lid on for 1 minute.

Line a large baking sheet (or two medium ones) with parchment paper. Tip the potatoes onto the sheet and space them apart. Use the back of a glass to squish each potato down until it cracks and flattens slightly. Drizzle with the olive oil and a pinch of salt and then roast in the oven for 35 minutes, or until golden and very crispy.

Now for your herby dressing. Tip the garlic into a bowl with the lemon juice and some salt. Stir in the herbs and capers along with the diced shallot and cover with the olive oil. Season to taste.

Meanwhile, put all the romesco ingredients into a high-speed blender and blitz until smooth.

Once the potatoes are cooked, you're ready to serve. Pick your favorite serving plate, pour the romesco sauce onto it, and swirl around the plate with the back of a spoon. Top with the crispy potatoes and a good drizzle of the herby dressing. Serve immediately to enjoy these crispy potatoes at their best!

SERVES 3 TO 4 AS A SIDE — GF

2 lb 2 oz / 1kg new potatoes
2 tbsp olive oil

FOR THE HERBY DRESSING

1 garlic clove, crushed to a paste
Juice of ½ lemon
1 tbsp chopped basil
1 tbsp chopped chives
1 tbsp chopped parsley
1 tbsp capers
½ shallot, finely diced
3 tbsp olive oil (or to cover)
Salt and black pepper

FOR THE ROMESCO SAUCE

100g blanched almonds
1 x 16 fl oz / 473ml jar roasted red bell peppers (about 12¾ oz / 360g drained weight)
1 garlic clove
1 tbsp nutritional yeast or freshly grated parmesan
1 tsp sherry vinegar (or red wine vinegar)
1 tsp olive oil
Pinch of salt

DESERT ISLAND DIPS

We've all heard of desert island dishes; well these are my desert island dips—four, to be precise! If there's one thing that gets eaten as fast as it gets made in our home it's hummus. It's the perfect snack, whether dipped into, smeared on a flatbread with pickles on top (a current fixation of mine), added to a sandwich, or served to kick things off at a dinner party. I've also included a bonus salty-sweet dip that just works and will get your guests talking to work out what it is.

THE ORIGINAL

Put the chickpeas into a food processor along with the tahini, garlic clove, lemon juice, and cumin and blitz. Add the water, bit by bit, until you reach a very smooth, slightly wet consistency. The hummus firms up in the fridge so don't be afraid to let it get loose.

Season with salt to taste and stir in the olive oil. I like to create swirls of oil on top and garnish with pine nuts, za'atar, sumac, or whatever I have available.

MAKES 1 BOWL — GF

2 x 15-oz / 425g cans good-quality chickpeas, drained and rinsed

3 tbsp tahini

1 garlic clove, peeled

Juice of ½ lemon

½ tsp ground cumin

½ to ¾ cup plus 2 tbsp / 100 to 200ml ice-cold water

2 tbsp olive oil

Pine nuts, za'atar, sumac, to serve (optional)

Salt

PESTO HUMMUS

Put the chickpeas into a food processor with the tahini, garlic, and lemon juice and blitz. Slowly add the ice water, bit by bit, until you reach a very smooth, slightly wet consistency. The hummus will firm up in the fridge so don't be afraid to let it get loose.

Season to taste and stir in the olive oil. Top with the pesto, swirling it in, and finish with the pine nuts.

MAKES 1 BOWL — GF

2 x 15-oz / 425g cans good-quality chickpeas, drained and rinsed

2 tbsp tahini

1 garlic clove

Juice of ½ lemon

½ to ¾ cup plus 2 tbsp / 100 to 200ml ice-cold water

2 tbsp olive oil

6 tbsp / 100g pesto (store-bought or page 212)

1 tbsp toasted pine nuts

Salt

ROASTED RED BELL PEPPER HUMMUS

Put the chickpeas, bell peppers, tahini, garlic, lemon juice, and smoked paprika into a food processor and blitz. Add the water, bit by bit, until you reach a very smooth, slightly wet consistency. The hummus firms up in the fridge so don't be afraid to let it get loose.

Season with salt to taste and stir in the olive oil. I like to create swirls of oil on top and scatter with pine nuts, more smoked paprika, oregano, or whatever I have available.

MAKES 1 BOWL — GF

2 x 15-oz / 425g cans good-quality chickpeas, drained and rinsed

Heaped 2 cups / 300g roasted red bell peppers from a jar

3 tbsp tahini

1 garlic clove

Juice of ½ lemon

1 tsp smoked paprika, plus more to garnish (optional)

½ to ¾ cup plus 2 tbsp / 100 to 200ml ice-cold water

2 tbsp olive oil

Pine nuts and oregano (fresh or dried), to serve (optional)

Salt

CORN AND FETA DIP

Bring a saucepan of water to a boil, add the corn, and cook for 3 to 4 minutes, then drain and set aside to cool.

Put the cooled corn into a food processor with the feta and garlic and blitz until fairly smooth. Season to taste and spread out on a plate. Top with the sliced green onion and chile and drizzle with the olive oil.

MAKES 1 BOWL — GF

Heaped 1 cup / 200g frozen corn kernels

2½ oz / 70g feta

1 garlic clove

1 green onion, sliced

1 red chile, sliced

1 tbsp olive oil

Salt and black pepper

SAUCES AND DRESSINGS

Having a few good sauces and dressings in your repertoire will enable you to think on your feet and create something spectacular with just a few simple ingredients; a good sauce or dressing can elevate even the simplest of dishes. This is why this is possibly the most useful chapter in the book. All these recipes can be made ahead of time and used to jazz up any odd bits and ends you have lying around in the fridge.

DAIRY-FREE CAESAR DRESSING

As I've already mentioned, I do love a Caesar salad.
I rarely use this sauce on anything but a Caesar-style
salad but it's definitely worth having in the repertoire.

Put the nuts, capers, mustard, and honey into a high-speed
blender and blitz until smooth, adding the water a little at a
time and stopping when you get the right consistency. Season
to taste and store in the fridge for 3 to 4 days.

SERVES 2 — GF

2 handfuls of cashews

1 tbsp capers

1 tsp Dijon mustard

1 tsp honey (or sweetener
of choice)

7 tbsp / 100ml water
(give or take)

Salt and black pepper

HOMEMADE PESTO

I'm well aware there are plenty of good store-bought
pestos out there, but making it fresh is always, always
worth it. Make it in a big vat and store the leftovers in
an ice-cube tray in the freezer and you have a portion
of pesto ready for whenever you need it.

Put all the ingredients except the olive oil into a blender and blitz
until roughly smooth (or use a mortar and pestle). Add the oil
slowly to reach your desired consistency; I prefer it to be slightly
loose. Season to taste and store in the fridge for 3 to 4 days.

MAKES APPROX.
1⅔ CUPS / 400G — GF

3 large handfuls of
fresh basil

1 garlic clove

Juice of ½ lemon

1 tbsp toasted pine nuts

1 heaped tbsp nutritional
yeast or freshly grated
parmesan

Olive oil

Salt and black pepper

ROMESCO SAUCE

This is so simple to make but whenever I serve it, people think I have made such an effort. All you need is a high-powered blender and you're good to go!

Put all the ingredients into a high-speed blender and blitz until smooth. Season to taste and store in the fridge for 3 to 4 days.

**MAKES APPROX.
2½ CUPS / 600G — GF**

¾ cup / 100g blanched almonds

1 x 16-fl oz / 473ml jar roasted red bell peppers, drained

1 garlic clove

1 tsp sherry vinegar

1 tbsp nutritional yeast or freshly grated parmesan

1 tsp olive oil

Pinch of salt

SPICY PINEAPPLE SALSA

A fruity salsa goes a long way in my book. The sweetness of the pineapple paired with the heat from the chile and tang from the onion works beautifully, and the creamy avocado ties it all together nicely.

Mix all the ingredients together in a bowl and season to taste. Store in the fridge for 2 to 3 days.

**MAKES APPROX.
2 CUPS / 500G — GF**

½ avocado, diced

½ red bell pepper, diced

½ red onion, finely diced

3 tbsp fresh pineapple, diced

3 tbsp frozen or fresh corn kernels

1 jalapeño, diced

1 garlic clove, finely chopped or grated

Juice of 2 limes

Handful of chives, chopped

Handful of cilantro, chopped

Salt and black pepper

213

SALTY CAPER AND HERB DRESSING

One of my all-time favorite dressings, this can take anything to the next level. Perfect with roasted veg, meat, fish—even tofu, for crying out loud! Do not sleep on this one!

Put the garlic into a bowl with the lemon juice and a pinch of salt and let sit while you chop the herbs as finely as possible. Add these to the bowl along with the chile and capers and pour in enough olive oil to cover. Season to taste and store in the fridge for 3 to 4 days.

MAKES APPROX. 1¼ CUPS / 300G — GF

1 small garlic clove, finely chopped or grated

Juice of ½ lemon

Big handful of parsley

Big handful of basil

Big handful of chives

1 red chile, diced

1 heaped tsp capers, roughly chopped

Olive oil, to cover

Salt and black pepper

SIMPLE DIJON VINAIGRETTE

Dijon vinaigrette is a classic and for good reason. It's tangy, sweet, and rich and makes the perfect accompaniment to salad leaves.

Put all the ingredients into a jar or bowl and shake or stir well. Season to taste and store in the fridge for 3 to 4 days.

MAKES APPROX. 1¼ CUPS / 300G — GF

1 small garlic clove, finely chopped or grated

Juice of ½ lemon

1 tsp Dijon mustard

1 tsp red wine vinegar

½ tsp honey

3 tbsp olive oil (or more as needed)

Salt and black pepper

PISTACHIO AND PARSLEY DRESSING

This is perfection with sweet vegetables such as squash, carrots, and sweet potato—the vibrant green contrasts perfectly with the orange vegetables and always looks beautiful on the plate.

Put the garlic into a bowl with the lemon juice and a pinch of salt and let sit while you roughly chop the pistachios and parsley. Add these to the bowl and pour in enough olive oil to cover. Season to taste and store in the fridge for 3 to 4 days.

MAKES APPROX. 1¼ CUPS / 300G — GF

1 small garlic clove, finely chopped or grated

Juice of ½ lemon

Handful of pistachios

Big handful of parsley

Olive oil, to cover

Salt and black pepper

HONEY MUSTARD DRESSING

Without a doubt, this is my most used dressing. Similar to the Dijon vinaigrette, it's undeniably a classic—it works on pretty much any salad!

Put all the ingredients into a jar or bowl and shake or stir well. Season to taste and store in the fridge for 3 to 4 days.

MAKES APPROX. 1¼ CUPS / 300G — GF

¼ cup / 60ml olive oil

1 tbsp whole-grain mustard

1 tbsp honey

Juice of 1 lemon

1 tbsp white wine vinegar

Salt and black pepper

MISO DRESSING

Miso is a wonderful ingredient—its rich, deep umami tones work with almost anything. I love to use it as a marinade for roasted tofu and eggplant, and the addition of honey makes the dressing turn sticky and sweet in the oven. It also works beautifully with salmon or cod.

Mix together the miso, sesame oil, rice wine vinegar, lemon juice, and honey and add a couple of splashes of cold water until a good dressing consistency is reached. Season to taste and store in the fridge for up to 1 week.

**MAKES APPROX.
1¼ CUPS / 300G — GF**

¼ cup / 65g white miso paste

¼ cup / 60ml sesame oil

2 tbsp rice wine vinegar

Juice of ½ lemon

1 tbsp honey (or sweetener of choice)

Cold water, as needed

Salt and black pepper

TAHINI DRESSING

Tahini really is like liquid gold. When you're buying it, look out for one that is very runny—it should not be solid! This dressing works so well with sweet, rich vegetables like squash, carrots, eggplant, and pumpkin. It has a sweet, creamy nuttiness that can perfectly balance out anything spicy.

Mix together the tahini, lemon juice, and honey, slowly adding a large spoonful or two of cold water to reach your desired consistency; I like mine quite thick. Season to taste and store in the fridge for 3 to 4 days.

**MAKES APPROX.
1¼ CUPS / 300G — GF**

3 tbsp tahini

Juice of ½ lemon

1 tsp honey

Cold water, as needed

Salt and black pepper

TANGY HERB DRESSING

Raw onion is not for everyone, but I would like to try and convert you with this dressing. The lemon juice and salt mellow the onion's intensity to provide the perfect tang to lift whatever it is you use this dressing on.

Put the garlic into a bowl with the lemon juice and a pinch of salt and let sit while you chop the onion and herbs as finely as possible. Add these to the bowl and top up with olive oil. Season to taste and store in the fridge for 3 to 4 days.

MAKES APPROX.
1¼ CUPS / 300G — GF

1 small garlic clove, finely chopped or grated

Juice of 1 lemon

½ red onion

Big handful of chives

Big handful of parsley

Big handful of basil

Olive oil, to cover

Salt and black pepper

SWEET THINGS

Although I am very much a savory girl, I do like to end
on a sweet note. Quite often at home after dinner, if we
don't have any freshly baked goods at the ready, you
will find me rooting through the snack cupboard looking
for something sugary to complete my evening meal.
Personally, I lean more toward either a fruity crumble
or a very naughty blondie/brownie/cookie situation, but
baking loaves, muffins, or cupcakes to give to friends
and family brings me great joy. There's no better feeling
than delivering freshly baked goods to someone's house
or handing them out to spontaneous guests at home
along with a hot cup of tea or coffee. This chapter is
filled with sweetness for all occasions.

ROASTED APRICOTS, CARDAMOM CREAM, AND PISTACHIO BRITTLE

This is a very simple but effective dessert. I like to serve this as a light summer dessert when perhaps the main meal has been on the heavy side. The pistachio brittle is totally addictive and stores well, so making a lot of it is always welcome.

Preheat the oven to 375°F and line two baking sheets with parchment paper.

Start by making the brittle. Put the sugar and water in a small saucepan over low heat. Bring to a boil, swirling the pan until the sugar has dissolved. Continue cooking the sugar for about 10 minutes—it will change color from light gold to deep amber. Watch it carefully so it doesn't burn—it's a fine line! Once it reaches this deep amber shade, remove from the heat and add the pistachios, stirring to coat the nuts, then pour onto one of the lined baking sheets while still malleable. Set aside to cool—it will need 15 to 20 minutes to fully set before you can crack it into pieces.

Next, place the apricot quarters on the other lined baking sheet. Pour the orange juice and honey over the top and mix well. Transfer to the oven and bake for 20 minutes, until tender. Let them cool for 15 minutes before serving.

While the apricots are in the oven, whisk together the cream and cardamom until a thick dropping consistency is reached.

Once the apricots have cooled, spoon a couple dollops of cream onto a small plate, create a well in the middle using the back of the spoon and then spoon a few apricots in, followed by a drizzle of their juices. Repeat for each portion. Top with the brittle and serve.

SERVES 4 — GF

6 apricots (plums also work), pitted and halved or quartered

Juice of ½ orange

1 heaped tbsp honey

FOR THE PISTACHIO BRITTLE

½ cup / 100g sugar

2 tbsp water

⅔ cup / 80g unsalted shelled pistachios, roughly chopped

FOR THE CREAM

¾ cup plus 2 tbsp / 200ml heavy cream of choice

½ tsp ground cardamom

MELT-IN-THE-MIDDLE BISCOFF AND BANANA MUFFINS

These feel so naughty and delicious—I absolutely love them. Biscoff is one of those things I tend to spoon straight out of a jar, especially when it's nearing my time of the month. Whoever made the executive decision to turn Lotus cookies into a spread deserves a Nobel Prize.

Preheat the oven to 375°F and line a 12-hole muffin pan with paper liners.

Begin by scooping 12 heaped teaspoons of Biscoff spread into small balls, then put them on a plate and pop into the freezer to set.

Make your egg replacement by mixing the ground flaxseed with the warm water in a small bowl. Set aside to thicken.

Mash the bananas in a large bowl, add the sugar and coconut oil, and whisk until combined. Add the flax egg (or egg) and mix well.

Combine the dry ingredients together in a separate bowl and then gently stir into the wet mixture until just combined; you are looking for a smooth batter but try not to overmix.

Check on the Biscoff balls—if they are solid enough to pick up, take them out of the freezer. Start layering up your muffins by scooping one large spoonful of batter into each muffin liner, then pop one Biscoff ball in the middle of each half-filled liner. Top the Biscoff balls with the remaining banana batter, making sure each ball is fully submerged.

Once all the batter has been poured into the liners, bake the muffins in the oven for 17 to 20 minutes, until golden. Let cool on a wire rack for 5 minutes before tucking in.

MAKES 12 MUFFINS

12 heaped tsp smooth Biscoff cookie butter

1 tbsp ground flaxseed (or 1 egg)

3 tbsp warm water

3 large very ripe bananas (10½ oz / 300g)

½ cup / 100g sugar

⅓ cup / 80ml coconut oil, melted

1 cup plus 3 tbsp / 150g all-purpose flour

½ cup / 50g almond flour (or use more all-purpose flour)

1 tsp baking soda

1 tsp baking powder

Pinch of salt

JEWELED TIFFIN

This is by far the easiest sweet to make in this book. It's a Christmas must in our house; we make a big batch and bash it up and you will always see someone nibbling on a piece. The recipe is definitely not exclusive to Christmas though, and you can totally customize the ingredients to your taste.

Start by lining a 9-inch / 23cm square baking pan with parchment paper.

Melt the chocolate in a bain-marie: fill a saucepan with 2 inches / 5cm of boiling water, put it over medium-low heat, and place a heatproof glass bowl on top, making sure the bottom does not touch the water. Break up the chocolate into the bowl and let it slowly melt.

Put the broken cookies, cranberries, pistachios, and macadamias into a separate bowl and then pour in two-thirds of the melted chocolate. Mix well and spread out into the lined pan. Top with the leftover melted chocolate to make a smooth top and finish with a sprinkle of sea salt.

Cover and place in the fridge for 2 hours or the freezer for 45 minutes, until solid.

Once set, break into random pieces and store in an airtight container.

TIP: To make this gluten free sub the Biscoff cookies with your favorite GF option—gingersnaps work really well.

SERVES 12 TO 14 — GFO

14 oz / 400g good-quality dark chocolate (70% cocoa solids) (or use milk chocolate if preferred)

1¾ oz / 50g broken Biscoff cookies

¼ cup / 25g dried cranberries

3 tbsp pistachios, roughly halved

3 tbsp macadamias, roughly halved

Flaky sea salt

HONEY, APRICOT, PECAN, AND PISTACHIO FLAPJACKS

In the UK, "flapjacks" refer to cereal bars, and these oaty squares of goodness are the perfect pick-me-up if you're experiencing that all too common mid-afternoon slump. The honey comes through so nicely and the combo of nuts and apricot gives them a lovely pop of color, crunch, and chewiness.

Preheat the oven to 300°F and grease and line a 9-inch / 23cm square baking pan with parchment paper.

Melt the butter in a saucepan over medium heat, then add the honey, sugar, and salt. Bring the mixture to a simmer, stirring until combined, and then simmer for 5 minutes, stirring regularly.

Mix all the dry ingredients together in a large bowl, then pour in the butter and honey mixture. Mix well to ensure all the oats are covered with the syrup before spreading the mixture into your lined pan. Flatten the surface into an even layer, taking care to scrape down the sides so that nothing burns in the oven. Use your hands or a spatula to press down firmly over the entire surface to compact the mixture. Bake for 45 to 50 minutes, until golden.

Once the flapjack has a good color, take it out of the oven, cover with a sheet of parchment paper, and place something heavy on top of the baked flapjack (still in the pan so that it keeps its shape). Let it cool down for at least 2 hours before slicing into squares.

TIP: Although oats don't naturally contain gluten, make sure to use GF oats if you are celiac.

MAKES 16 SQUARES
— GFO

1 cup plus 2 tbsp / 250g unsalted butter (or vegan alternative), plus extra for greasing

3 heaped tbsp honey

Packed ½ cup / 100g light brown sugar

Pinch of sea salt

⅔ cup / 65g pecans, roughly chopped

½ cup / 65g pistachios, roughly chopped

1¼ cups / 150g dried apricots, chopped

3¾ cups / 350g rolled oats

BLUEBERRY AND BANANA MUFFINS

Blueberry and banana muffins are the height of nostalgia for me—in fact, I find anything with bananas is nostalgic because when I was a child, the only time my mum ever spontaneously baked was when we had browning bananas hanging around. These, in particular, remind me of living with my brother. They were on an almost weekly rotation and he would eat at least two a day.

Preheat the oven to 375°F and line a 12-hole muffin pan with paper liners.

Make your egg replacement by mixing the ground flaxseed with the warm water in a small bowl. Set aside to thicken.

Mash the bananas in a large bowl, add the sugar and coconut oil, and whisk until combined. Add the flax egg (or egg) and mix well.

Combine the dry ingredients in a separate bowl and then gently combine them with the wet mixture along with the blueberries. Try not to overmix; stir until just combined.

Scoop the batter evenly into the muffin liners and sprinkle the tops with the oats for decoration. Bake in the oven for 17 to 20 minutes, or until the tops are golden. Remove and then let cool on a wire rack for 5 minutes before tucking in.

TIP: The almond flour used here creates a very moist muffin and it works in most cake or muffin recipes!

MAKES 12 MUFFINS

1 tbsp ground flaxseed (or 1 egg)

3 tbsp warm water

3 large very ripe bananas (10½ oz / 300g)

½ cup / 100g sugar

⅓ cup / 80ml coconut oil, melted

1 cup plus 3 tbsp / 150g all-purpose flour

½ cup / 50g almond flour (or use more all-purpose flour)

1 tsp baking soda

1 tsp baking powder

1½ cups / 250g blueberries

¼ cup / 20g rolled oats, for the top

Pinch of salt

CARAMELIZED PECAN, CHOCOLATE, AND BANANA BREAD

As I said before, banana baked goods are hugely nostalgic for me. We obviously didn't eat enough bananas when they were fresh because we always had brown ones lying around that were then whipped up into some sort of banana loaf or muffin! The caramelized pecans give this a lovely crunch and if you eat a slice warm out of the oven, the pools of melted chocolate make it totally irresistible.

Preheat the oven to 375°F and line a 9 × 5-inch / 900g loaf pan with parchment paper.

Start by preparing your flax egg: stir together the ground flaxseed and warm water and set aside to thicken.

To caramelize the pecans, toss them in the maple syrup and cinnamon and then pop onto a baking sheet lined with parchment paper. Bake in the oven for 8 minutes, keeping an eye on them so that they don't burn. Set aside to cool.

Mash the bananas in a large bowl, then whisk in the sugar and coconut oil. Stir in the flax egg, then add the chocolate and caramelized pecans.

Combine the all-purpose flour, almond flour, baking soda, and baking powder in a separate bowl and then gently stir into the wet mixture. When fully combined, pour the mixture into the lined loaf pan, ensuring that it is even on top. Bake in the oven for 45 to 50 minutes, until just cooked but golden on top.

Remove from the oven and let cool on a wire rack. Sprinkle some flaky sea salt on top to really bring it to life.

TIP: I love to eat mine with a slathering of butter.

MAKES 1 LOAF

2 tbsp ground flaxseed

3 tbsp warm water

½ cup / 50g pecans, roughly chopped

1 tbsp maple syrup

1 tsp ground cinnamon

3 large very ripe bananas (10½ oz / 300g)

½ cup / 100g sugar

⅓ cup / 80ml coconut oil, melted

3½ oz / 100g dark chocolate, chopped into big chunks

1 cup plus 3 tbsp / 150g all-purpose flour

½ cup / 50g almond flour (or use more all-purpose flour)

1 tsp baking soda

1 tsp baking powder

Pinch of flaky sea salt

235

DARK CHOCOLATE CHUNK AND SEA SALT COOKIES

When I was about fourteen I spent two days making countless batches of cookies, trying to perfect my recipe. I then had to retest it when I began cutting eggs and dairy from my diet and this was the result: chewy in the middle, crisp around the edges, and loaded with chocolate. I love the salty-sweet combo, so adding a good pinch of salt to them when they're fresh out of the oven is a must.

Preheat the oven to 375°F and line 2 baking sheets with parchment paper.

In a large bowl, beat together the butter and sugars for about 2 minutes until light and fluffy—I like to use an electric mixer for this bit. Add the milk and vanilla and whisk again.

Using a wooden spoon, mix in the flour, baking powder, and baking soda. Roughly chop the chocolate into big chunks and add these too, then use your hands to knead the mixture so it comes together well. Pop the mixture into the fridge for 15 minutes to firm up.

Once the dough has cooled and your oven has heated up, you can start laying out the cookie dough balls. Divide the dough into 12 equal-size balls (about 2 oz / 55g per ball). Place them on the lined baking sheets, making sure they have at least 3 inches / 7cm between them to spread—they grow!

Bake in the oven for 10 to 15 minutes, until golden around the edges. Sprinkle the tops with a little sea salt and then let cool for 10 minutes to firm up before digging in!

MAKES 12 COOKIES

½ cup / 110g butter
(or vegan alternative)

Packed ⅔ cup / 150g light brown sugar

¼ cup plus 1 tbsp / 60g granulated sugar

2 tbsp milk of choice

1 tsp vanilla bean paste or extract

1½ cups / 200g all-purpose flour

½ tsp baking powder

½ tsp baking soda

3½ oz / 100g good-quality dark chocolate (or as much as you want)

Flaky sea salt, for sprinkling

APPLE GALETTE WITH MISO CARAMEL SAUCE

This is the type of dessert that looks like you've made so much more effort than you have. It's classic, elegant, and absolutely delicious. You could, of course, make your own pastry from scratch, but let's be real, we don't always have time for that. Scoop up some apples (any variety you like) and pie crust from the grocery store and the rest I'm sure you'll find in the pantry!

Preheat the oven to 375°F and line a large baking sheet with parchment paper.

Put the apple slices into a mixing bowl with the flour, brown sugar, and lemon juice. Give everything a good mix.

Unroll one crust (reserve the other for a different recipe) straight onto the lined baking sheet and cut out a 10-inch / 25cm circle about 1/16-inch / 2mm thick (use a dinner plate as a guide). Arrange the apples in a pattern, leaving a 1-inch / 2.5cm border, then fold the edges in to slightly overlap the fruit and brush with milk. Sprinkle a pinch more sugar around the edges of the pastry so that they get a nice color and bake for 20 to 25 minutes, or until golden around the edges.

Meanwhile, make the caramel. Put the sugar and water into a saucepan and set over low heat. Swirl the saucepan occasionally to encourage the sugar to melt evenly but do not stir! Once the sugar has melted, turn the heat up and let the mixture come to a gentle boil. Simmer for 8 to 10 minutes, watching it like a hawk so it doesn't burn. Once it turns a rich amber color, remove it from the heat and whisk in the butter and cream. It will bubble and splatter so be careful! Whisk in the miso and let the caramel cool for 10 minutes before serving, drizzled on top of the galette.

TIP: Vanilla ice cream will always be a welcome addition, and you can make this gluten free by using GF pie crust and flour.

SERVES 4 TO 6 — GFO

2 to 3 large apples (10½ oz / 300g), cored and sliced into 1/16-inch / 2mm slices

1 heaped tbsp all-purpose flour

Packed ¼ cup / 50g brown sugar, plus extra for sprinkling

Juice of ½ lemon

1 x 14.1-oz / 400g package of pre-rolled pie crust

2 tbsp milk of choice

FOR THE MISO CARAMEL

¾ cup / 150g granulated sugar

¼ cup / 60ml water

1½ tbsp unsalted butter (or vegan alternative), cubed

⅔ cup / 160ml heavy cream of choice

½ heaped tbsp white miso paste

RHUBARB, GINGER, AND CARDAMOM CRUMBLE

A crumble must have a good level of tartness and rhubarb never fails to hit the spot. This is fragrant, floral, and fruity and the perfect crowd-pleaser.

Preheat the oven to 375°F.

Put the rhubarb into an 8-inch / 20cm square or similar size ovenproof dish and sprinkle with the ginger and brown sugar. Squeeze the orange juice over the top and give everything a good mix.

In a separate bowl, mix together the flour, butter, and brown sugar, using your fingers to create a sand-like texture. Mix the oats in at the end.

Using your hands, sprinkle the mixture across the rhubarb, gently squeezing small clumps together and then patting them in to create satisfying chunks of crumble. Bake in the oven for 25 to 30 minutes, until golden on top.

Meanwhile, pour the cream into a bowl and sprinkle in the powdered sugar and the ground cardamom. Whisk until just thickened and holding its shape. Set in the fridge until the crumble is ready.

Once the crumble is golden, remove from the oven and let cool for 5 minutes so that the crumble top can harden. Serve with big dollops of the cream.

TIP: Use GF flour and oats to make this gluten free.

SERVES 6 — GFO

4 to 5 stalks of rhubarb (14 oz / 400g), cut into 1¼-inch / 3cm pieces

2-inch / 5cm piece of ginger, grated

7 tbsp / 85g light brown sugar

Juice of 1 large orange

FOR THE CRUMBLE

1⅓ cups / 160g all-purpose flour

6 tbsp / 80g cold butter (or vegan alternative), cut into cubes

7 tbsp / 85g light brown sugar

½ cup / 50g rolled oats

FOR THE CREAM

¾ cup plus 2 tbsp / 200ml heavy cream of choice

1 tbsp powdered sugar, sifted

½ tsp ground cardamom

CHAI-SPICED CHOCOLATE AND PECAN BLONDIES

The spices that go into chai are just so wholesome and warming; they work perfectly in this bake. These blondies are gooey in the middle, almost cookie-like around the edges, and totally irresistible. You won't be able to stop eating them!

Preheat the oven to 350°F and line a 9-inch / 23cm square baking pan with parchment paper.

Melt the butter in a saucepan, then put it into a bowl with both sugars and whisk until the sugar has almost completely melted into the butter. Pour in the milk and vanilla and beat until combined.

Add the flour, baking soda, spices, and salt and fold until the mixture is almost all combined, then add the chocolate chunks along with the pecans.

Transfer the mixture to the lined pan, smoothing out the top with a spatula. Bake for 20 to 22 minutes, until golden; it should still have a slight wobble when you take it out of the oven but fear not, it will set as it cools. Let cool for 20 minutes on a wire rack before cutting into squares.

MAKES 16 SQUARES

¾ cup / 160g butter (or vegan alternative)

Packed ⅔ cup / 140g light brown sugar

¼ cup plus 1 tbsp / 60g granulated sugar

3 tbsp milk of choice

1 tsp vanilla bean paste

1½ cups / 200g all-purpose flour

½ tsp baking soda

1 tsp ground cinnamon

½ tsp ground ginger

¼ tsp grated nutmeg

¼ tsp ground cardamom

Pinch of salt

3½ oz / 100g good-quality dark chocolate (ideally 70% cocoa solids), roughly chopped

¾ cup / 80g pecans, roughly chopped

ACKNOWLEDGMENTS

There are many people that have been so instrumental in my life and in leading to the creation of this book. The first person I would like to thank is my mum, to whom this book is dedicated. You have always been my biggest cheerleader and supported me through every phase of my life, regardless of whether you agreed with it or not. Without your unconditional love (and home-cooked meals), life would be very different. You inspire me every day—thank you.

Gary, you have made me fall in love with the term "father figure"; thank you for your endless love, support, and savvy business advice. Having you back my corner has given me the confidence to seize any and all opportunities in life. I couldn't be more grateful for you.

Thank you to Cameron, my fiancé, for just being amazing. It is hard to put into words how much you mean to me. Thank you for being the most incredible sounding board, therapist, food sampler, and life partner; I literally could not have done this without you. I love you very, very much.

Thank you to Thomas, Nikolai, Daniel, Phil, and all my wonderful friends and family for always being so unbelievably encouraging and supportive. You know who you are.

I am so grateful for the community of foodies I have been introduced to since becoming a recipe content creator, but especially grateful to Elly, Issy, Clare, and Soph for all of the support, love, and friendship. It would be lonely without you!

Thank you to all my clients! Thank you for the advice, the adventures, the encouragement, and the friendship. I will always look back at our time together with warmth and fondness.

A huge thank you to Ludo and Eve from the Eve White agency and the whole team at Penguin Life for believing in me when I wasn't so sure and for making me feel so safe and looked after throughout this whole process. A special thanks to Amy for dealing with my terrible grammar, testing all my recipes, and for the countless hours spent rifling through the manuscript and making it what it is today. Thank you to Dickie, Bonnie, and Amelia for bringing the pages to life!

I would like to say thank you to Issy, Emily, and Joe for being the most incredible shoot team. I could not have asked for a better group of people to work alongside. Issy, the way you have captured the food is exactly how I imagined it, only better. Emily, your eye for styling is simply perfection and I have learned so much from you. And Joe, your music and cooking skills are *chef's kiss.* Thank you for making me feel so comfortable and welcome in the studio, and for all the laughs.

Thank you to James, Good City Agency, and Kayla for all the hard work, but more importantly, for the friendship and for helping me become a full-time creator.

Finally, the biggest thank you to each and every single person who has followed my @natsnourishments account, re-created and shared my recipes, and supported me on this wild online journey. Without you, none of this would have happened, and for that I am eternally grateful. And a big thank you to my good friend Tom, who thought up the name "Nat's Nourishments."

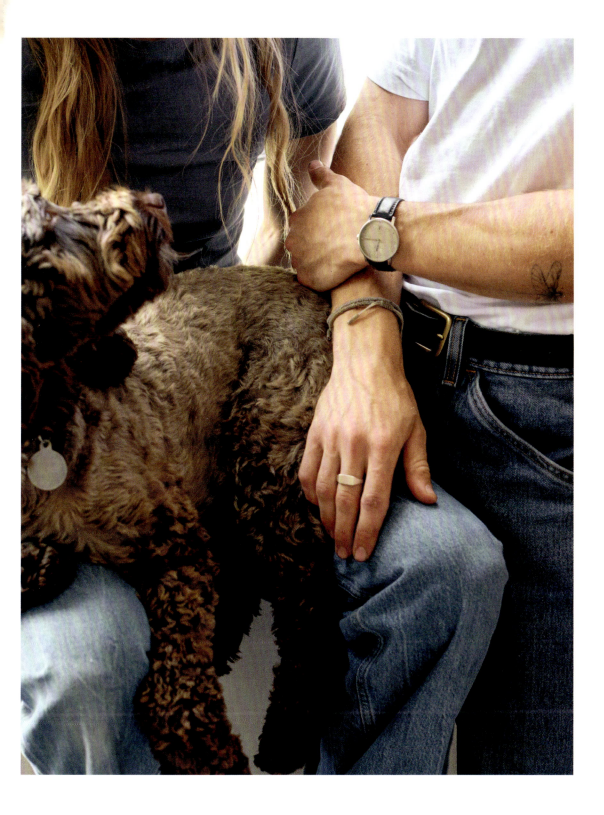

INDEX

Ten Speed Press
An imprint of the Crown Publishing Group
A division of Penguin Random House LLC
1745 Broadway
New York, NY 10019
tenspeed.com
penguinrandomhouse.com

First published in 2025 by Penguin Life, an imprint of Penguin General. Penguin General is
part of the Penguin Random House group of companies.

Typefaces: Monotype's Plantin and Bitstream's Swiss 721

Library of Congress Cataloging-in-Publication Data is on file with the publisher.

Hardcover ISBN: 978-0-593-83660-6
Ebook ISBN: 978-0-593-83661-3

Acquiring editor: Kelly Snowden | Project editor: Cristina Garces
Production editor: Natalie Blachere | Editorial assistant: Kausaur Fahimuddin
Production designers: Mari Gill and Mara Gendell
Production: Jane Chinn
Americanizer: Maria Zizka
Proofreaders: Pat Dailey, Erica Rose, and Andrea Connolly Peabbles
Publicist: Kristin Casemore | Marketer: Brianne Sperber

Manufactured in China

10 9 8 7 6 5 4 3 2 1

First North American Edition

The authorized representative in the EU for product safety and compliance is Penguin
Random House Ireland, Morrison Chambers, 32 Nassau Street, Dublin D02 YH68, Ireland,
https://eu-contact.penguin.ie.